D0886520

HOLDFAST

POEMS

Christian Anton Gerard

C&R Press
Conscious & Responsible

First Edition
1 2 3 4 5 6 7 8 9

Selections of up to two pages may be reproduced without permissions. To reproduce more than two pages of any one portion of this book write to C&R Press publishers John Gosslee and Andrew Sullivan.

Cover Art by Eugenia Loli
Cover Design by C&R Press

Library of Congress Cataloging-in-Publication Data

ISBN: 978-1-936196-74-6
LCCN: 2017943610

C&R Press
Conscious & Responsible
www.crpress.org

For special discounted bulk purchases please contact:
C&R Press sales@crpress.org

For Michael C. Peterson, Terry Loum and Clynch Varnadore

HOLDFAST

CONTENTS

Part 1

The Poet Making a Scene   7

Whiskey Called. She Said,   9

Irises   10

Pointed   11

Steelhead Don't Ask Where the White Goes   12

For a Poet Who Fears His Elegies Are Too Sentimental   14

Twenty-Something Poet Made a Mix Tape   15

Rhinoceri Believe in a Golden Age for Love   16

[Because there are nights that seem to put one arm first]   18

Image   20

Materials; or Revision   21

Operator's Manual   22

Usable Past   24

Permission   26

Vocabulary   27

Anonymous   28

Christian Anton Gerard to Scalise from New Orleans   30

To Ansel on His Second Birthday   32

Poem with Madrigals   34

Still Life with Myself Two Years Six Months Sober   35

Part 2

Defense of Poetry; or The Poet Explaining Himself   39

Poetry Can Save the World?   40

Defense of Poetry; or Prayer in Recovery   41

Defense of Poetry; or Alcoholic Expected Home   43

Ars Poetica   44

Water Skiing with Robert Creeley   45

Defense of Poetry; or Love Prayer Prayed by Christian Anton Gerard   46

Defense of Poetry   47

Christian Anton Gerard Thinking He's Milton's Adam   48

Sublime Prayer for an Alcoholic   49

Confession of the Alcoholic Poet Who Brought Books into a Public Restroom   50

[You've seen him looking up from the table]   52

Blood Is No More Life than a Cloud Resembling a Goose Is a Goose   54

Pastoral Instinct of a Recovered Alcoholic   56

A Knife's Signature in His Alcoholic Palms   57

Pastoral: Can We Say Cowboy Anymore?   59

Defense of Poetry; or Poem with Bowling Leagues and Black Dresses 61
Poet Seeing Stars 62
Or Dear John Ashbery, 63
Defense of Poetry; or Poem in which I Can't Imagine My Own Death 64
Aubade in Afternoon 66
Christian Anton Gerard Is Unable To Be Opaque 67
Holdfast: My Alcoholic Head in Recovery 69
Tonight the Space You Need 70
Christian Anton Gerard, a Shearsman of Sorts 71
Sobering Interrogative: A Man's Most Vulnerable 72
Christian Anton Gerard Reads Her 73
Christian Anton Gerard Moving Toward Psalm 75
Defense of Poetry; or The Alcoholic's Imitation 77
Defense Prayer 78

Part 3

Enargeia 81
Christian Anton Gerard and Her Yet without a Past 82
Her and Christian Anton Gerard in an Argon Cloud 83
Defense of Poetry; or How To Say the Heart's Epitome 84
You Poem You 86
Asylum Seeker Driving through Northwest Arkansas 88
Preservation 89
Christian Anton Gerard to Her Sort of in the Style of a Teenaged Love Poem 90
Dear Bob Dylan I'm Not Angry 92
Poem with Pursed Lips 93
Christian Anton Gerard to Ryan Adams via Caliban 94
Christian Anton Gerard to Josh Jones 95
Christian Anton Gerard to Her 96
Dear You, Ideally It Will Go Down Like This: 97
Christian Anton Gerard in the Introspective 99
Notes 100

Acknowledgements 106

1

The Poet Making a Scene

Two boys are practice-dancing shirtless
on the lawn. A bicycle is chained to a rack for bikes.

People fill the quad like they know what they're doing.
One guy's in the middle of it all with a video camera.

He's turning in circles like a narrator.
I raise my hand and he raises his almost

like a flinch at first. He wonders if he knows me. He doesn't.
Now he's packing his camera, moving on

as if I'd taken something away. I am Spenser's Calidore
up in arms. I am Calidore the hunter telling Artegall, *but where*

ye ended have, now I begin to tread an endless
trace, withouten guyde or good direction how

to enter in, or how to issue forth in waies untryde
In perils strange, in labours long and wide. I am

not Calidore inserting myself into the world without
regard for the world of which I'm part. I have a father

and so acknowledge his father-ness in questing for a gift
to celebrate his part in my world, to understand him, a maker

fathered by his father and all the fathers before him.
I see the shirtless boys practice-dancing, see them making

love to each other, the dance, the ways a body moves—
A lyric. A narrative. The art hiding itself so

emotion bellows out, filling a moment
with what never before has filled a moment.

I am not Calidore without a guide or good direction.
I have Spenser, Calidore's maker, and all the poets between us.

I called both Hallmarks in town and neither has
the frame I wanted for Father's Day. I have Spenser,

though, his own allegory, to show me I am
my own allegory, to help me see the heart's racing in,

stumbling. How intricate to acknowledge the enough,
the vigilance required to stay hidden and then admit.

Whiskey Called. She Said,

her name. Christian Anton Gerard can still,
God grant him, taste his tongue that last time
he had her: on the walnut table,
the chairs, in that blue room warm and cold.
Bold and bolder, Whiskey telling
Christian, come. Come *inside*.

How Christian stood in that room, a place like feeling,
a place like infinity. No.
Whiskey ate its tail inside him.

Inside him. *Inside*. She said where
he needed to go: Inside you, she said, and not
soul-searching Christian, you can't
search for what's somewhere in a locked room
throwing itself at walls
worn now to metal rivets throat-burn bare,

its teeth broken trying
to bite off the rivets, to break out of this
room I've made inside you. Inside

Christian was like that blue room
where a family could sit to eat, put together
that jigsaw puzzle amid the rolling hills
Christian said he'd roll down with his son.

But in his blue room—Whiskey's voice
like salt in a hillside, gold in river dust, Whiskey's
timbre saying everything he could see, almost.
How he wished to walk the river, go inside the hillside.
Christian walked the line. Whiskey walked him in.

Irises

—and the wisdom to know the difference

I think therefore I am a problem. Christian
you are a problem for you. Most
of your problems are you, your making.
Melancholy. Sometimes I live there and love it.
Christian, you love to live. Confess it.

Anne Sexton lived her label. That room.
Christian, you became a man in rooms
around tables. Let yourself be, Christian.

Thinking of Matthew Dickman's line
"I want to be good to myself." You want to be
good to yourself. I'm afraid I am.
I go to rooms with tables. I confess my name.
You do. Why do you?
Because I'm a confession uncathartic.

Carthasis is for tragedy. I have been my own. Everyone's
story if said a certain way. Christian, can you empathize
with yourself? If I do, I'm proud—a blue light
toward flitbumble hungry. Kind of. Christian,
what have you learned
of the blues? The blues are not

melancholy. Blue is not. Blues are hope capitalized.
Hope. Look at it, Christian. Hope. Look at that. What color
is that word? Your eyes, Christian, are Hope.
Not if I'm blue-streaked proud.
If Blue is Hope or Hope is, then what are your eyes? What I've looked for

to look with.
What are they? Do you want to be
good to yourself? Yes. I confess.
Where are you, Christian?
On my knees. In this night.
How do you know? My Hope is open.

Pointed

—the courage to change the things I can

The middle ground is the fear Christian faces
in her eyes when in the afternoon he sees himself
there in those green irises in their red bed in their
red room. She has taught him to hold red on his tongue,
his teeth, the cliffs from which he's jumped so many times
like the man who jumped from Bill Wilson's second story

window 'cause he couldn't face himself—a mattress afire
falling in the night—a different conception of shooting star.
In the middle ground, Christian is a burning mattress
heart-brain with a copper pipe in its embers—*Aurora
Borealis* held in his skull's silver chalice, and the broken
owning his image in her eyes.

My brain is broken
compared to most of my readers. This is neither self-
deprecation nor self-pity's well, reader. This is me
reading too. These words are seventeen generals meeting
in the middle of seventeen thousand slain women and men
saying goodbye to this life on grass, guns, the legs, hips, chests

of friends and enemies, many of whom are both.
If the generals do it right, they will want
to say peace is possible in this place long as they can,
but they'll be able to agree there's only this grass today.
Perhaps there's only today—seventeen thousand souls
proving all their fears. How could they all fall on their own

swords, gleaming like their love's eyes, admitting
there's no proof the sun will rise if night's not run through.
There's always a point, sharp as a hellhound's canines,
and the point, like staring at a single ember, can and will
run riot through my sternum, between my lungs
and show itself where my *latissimus dorsi* meet—

my own middle ground. I am, will be,
like the sword in the stone, except you will not see a hilt
nor a handle. Those are buried beneath me. But you
will see the point and know if you grab it, blood
will run from your hands. You will look at them, wonder
why on earth? I have asked myself the same.

Steelhead Don't Ask Where the White Goes

—the serenity to accept the things I cannot change

Vein figure. Right forearm. Pitch-
fork. There's blood in there. There's nine
circles in there. There, there. There,
there. Sometimes I need my sweet
        slow cry time. Left forearm. A
river's mouth. A salmon run.
There's something in there calls the
heart home. There, there. Heart, I swear.
        Sometimes I need my river
mouth crying sign. September
Fifteen Two Thousand Twelve. Where
my walkway ends, tees into
        the sidewalk. No crossroads. No
walkaways. No. There. It was
there. I could stand. I stood. I
couldn't drive. Had driven. There,
        there. There, there I stood both arms
above my head. That crying
time. Shirt on my back, then no.
There, September. There, kissing
        sun kissing the coming night.
That old kissing game. Once a
black dress. One night white satin.
Once, nothing but a tree's trunk
        in my hands. There, September
Fifteen Two Thousand Twelve I
felt that evening kissing game.
All those eves. There, there ride four
        horsemen under my shirt. Shirt
on my back, then no. Took it
off. Shirt like skin. Shirt as skin.
My skin. There, thinner than a
        tear's voice. There, these eyes singing
litanies. My own gospels.
There, there. There, there. The song in
this wannabe cowboy's cry

time. Steelhead don't ask where the
white goes when the snow's gone. They
just go there. There where they'll give
until their hearts give out. There
        they go. September Fifteen
Two Thousand Twelve. I was
there. My own river's mouth. Those
veins. My pitchfork's blood-lined tines.

For a Poet Who Fears His Elegies Are Too Sentimental

This winter has weighed and
judged you, Michael, told you you cannot
escape your mother's death, the poems

in which she lives and is gone already.
This winter has swaddled you
in brown paper sweaters, made you

eat of yourself from your own store
when you've spent every penny buying
yourself from yourself, then stealing.

Aren't we always damning the seasons
for making us thieve ourselves? This winter
married you, though—its own

kind of season—in which you must steal
from yourself to give all of yourself or
so is said. I told my wife she was everything.

She said she is not my skin or the air,
that she couldn't feed me without food.
I've hated her and loved her more for that.

We knew ourselves first as sons, then husbands—
not preferencing here, just chronological truth.
This winter's kept you honest about boy-poets' burdens

in the weather of the internal universe. This winter,
then, because syntax, expectation, is heavy,
because my elegy for yours is less elegy,

more praise, for your trying to say. This winter
I believe it's possible for boy poets to be
born and raised on the words we need.

Twenty-Something Poet Made a Mix Tape

I cut my hair with a knife so I could be a knight.
        I went to the river so I would smell like a man
who can handle the whole world. I was
        a knight with a lion's hunger, a bull elephant's
thirst. She kneeled on one knee. Will you,
        Christian Anton Gerard, take me to bed?
I asked if she loved me.
        She asked if I'd made a mix tape.
Yes, I said, and she said yes. I had built
        the music box whose one song sung
the sound a deer makes lapping
        the river's edge; the song born of Aphra Behn and
Whitman, perfected by PM Dawn and Prince, Otis
        Redding, Michael Jackson, Madonna. We made out
like teenagers in the hallway. We were *Rent's*
        "No Day But Today" and *West Side Story's* "Maria."
We sang all the mix tape's songs—songs written by
        knights and ladies for the kind of night happening once
a knight trades armor and opponents for the dance-
        floor and feasting the movies and old books make
tilt or battle days out to be. Everything accorded
        to the laws of boys afraid we might have sex.
She and I sang songs of ourselves. We stopped
        singing long enough for me to grope my pocket
for protection, then we sang again. We were
        housesitting for our professor, his teen son
slapped me five on his way out; she was on her way in.
        The old condom-in-the-palm transfer, a practice
between brothers of a certain shield, boy-law's bylaws.
        She and I were set to be spinning dancers on the night's
music box wound for the long song, the longest song
        imaginable. I took a chance on a solo, but screamed soliloquy.
I couldn't feel her or me. The play no longer the thing,
        why boys are afraid of nights like that. I was
a b-boy bucking. She flicked the light on. Said,
        she'd never seen a thin-sized condom. I hadn't
believed in karma till then, till I saw myself
        reduced to black and blue—Purple Rain's apologetics.
She got some ice and her poetry anthology.
        She read Rochester's "Imperfect Enjoyment," then
Donne and Wyatt, excerpts from *Paradise Lost.*
        Quintessential lovers, she said, are always fucked,
the trying to love, a fiasco bigger than love itself.

Rhinoceri Believe in a Golden Age for Love

We can agree there's a time for honesty
and then there's a time for honesty.
This is one of those times. Honestly,

that night on my parents' roof after
we'd bought the condoms and made
our pacts and you asked if I was ready

I said yes, that I was all yours, but
I didn't tell you I couldn't quit thinking of
the National Geographic I'd perused

that morning in the can, the rhinoceri
about to die from drought so I herded them
from Africa into my virginity's history.

I've come to know them as the way
I know something important's going
to happen, go out the window, or jump a horse.

And again they're here in this, doing
whatever rhinos do when they aren't dying.
I've burnt up shadows staring into myself,

the sun on the Serengeti. I thought you
a sky alive with birds of paradise, even
when the rhinoceri first came to me and

even when afterward you said I couldn't love,
not really, because we were seventeen.
I wasn't angered by your words til now,

drinking on a street café's deck. I am
sitting with friends, a man and a woman.
Another woman walks up to sit with us.

The new woman offers herself to my friend
        who promptly says my other friend is his
girlfriend. The new woman lowers her price.

        Bellowing rhinos surround me, rhinos
not dying of drought. The new woman understands,
        starts to stand to leave, but falls over,

drunk in the road. She refuses my hand
        to help her up, out of shame, mine or hers,
who knows. The rhinos are here and charging

        for the grace a boy in love deserved. Rhinoceri
believe in a golden age for love. The new
        woman tells my friends no one can buy

what she saw between them, she's tried
        for years to drink her heart's lake. I want
to say I scooped her up, a silver stallion

        crossing the plain, herding the rhinos, that
there was no time to fashion a saddle
        or make declarations in the night,

that we and the rhinos set off for every mirage.

[Because there are nights that seem to put one arm first]

on a ladder toward day

and then a foot back on the ground as if
the indecision's deeper than definitive.
Because we learn first to smile in sleep before

the lips carve out the inside in daylight. Because
daylight can be carved out of the mind, as in

a silhouette, my son's.
There is his mouth, which cannot say a word,
but works against the light, a stage's scrim, as if

the inside were a chorus chanting low harmonies
barely hearable, bearable, less audible than palpable,

the curtain pulling back to show the players playing
and the players playing their own thanks.
I've talked for years about essay as a derivative

of assay—to talk—as if the essay were a conversation,
a response to something else external, but Montaigne

meant *essais* as *attempts*—take away
the thesis, take away the logic and rhetoric,
strip away what's thought-through and there is only

that thing felt, maybe even before the feeling
becomes an idea. I hope

flowers are flags of happiness, like smiles,
that from a distance are bright as trying
to make poems on a dark sea that's never dark

except to those who've imagined
their way into light.

I gave my ex-wife a dozen yellow roses
before she was my wife, before I knew
I loved her because I believed I would love her.

I didn't know Aristotle believed a smile showed the soul.
My son sits sleeping in his mother's arms

against the window's light and something pulls to one side his lip,
suggesting something's right in there.
I used to think flowers were fireworks celebrating

the dark not eating me. I've wanted tonight
to describe my son's smile. I've watched him sleep for hours.

Image

If I was honest with myself, I'd be able to admit
I wish Whitman's portrait could be my self-portrait,

that Whitman's ghost is real as me.
Some months back I read Whitman was obsessed

with pictures produced by a camera. The machine
able to capture a moment's difference in a man.

Tonight my wife and I hung the bird feeders
my mother gave us, who loves birds, who

often takes pictures of those both rare and not-so-rare-
appearing little visions in the yard.

Many birders handle the hobby in like manner.
I suspect my wife and I also will.

Our pictures will try so hard to make clear
we know a moment's value, the breath-taking startle

scuttled by a scarlet warbler or the ping-pong-ball-tailed wren's
happy-go-lucky-ho-hum-hop-around-the-porch morning. Perhaps

the oriole won't return next year. The blue bird might
find a better store of shelled, halved, peanuts. If I was

honest with myself, I'd admit the moment's difference in me—
Boy to man, man to man, neither's held in winged ghost stories.

I've no photo albums filled with birds. Love's not a hobby
with stories like the pileated woodpecker who flew before

the shutter's click, flash changing everything. It's fall
now. My wife's no longer my wife. Years turn

to Kodacolored flames. Black and White. Color.
Negative and capability. Tonight's indiscriminate fire.

Materials; or Revision

Desire is no price haggler, so when they found that rust-bucket truck and drove deep into each other, that bed, their hauled bodies, they found that peering-through-for-sale-pages-feeling. Christian Anton Gerard didn't expect that next morning to wake and wordlessly re-receive his grandfather's hammer from her in red satin ribbon, the one given him to build a workbench, a book shelf, a house to house a family, or rather, to make his house fit his family. She and Christian Anton Gerard had been like Frost's "Home Burial" couple. How they'd beat each other with misunderstandings, breaths smaller than the words required to build them—Love, she was saying in the giving, is the history of its repurposing.

Operator's Manual

The UPS man should be here by now
with the rotary tool attachment I sent away for by email.

I have tracked the parcel, paced kitchen to the porch,
sat cross-legged in my green vintage La-Z-Boy pretending

to read Nabokov's *Pnin*. The first ten pages
are excellent writing. John Updike's right: "ecstatic prose."

Pnin's the kind of guy you drink tequila with and go TP Old Man Smith's yard
because he's always out in his garage building things
I plan to build when my rotary tool attachment arrives.

My rotary tool is a Dremel.
The attachment is a small router table.

Sure, I've built shelves before (one strong enough to hold a microwave),
but when the router arrives I'll be rounding my edges, grooving and shaping
like a drunk's shadow across alley walls
on the kind of night feeling like Bob Seger had everything right.

I once drove across America with an ex-professional bowler turned
bucket-truck mechanic.

Somewhere in Utah's deserts he said he met Seger
in the Seventies right after *Night Moves'* release.
Seger's tour bus caravan stopped for service
at the RV shop where Tom was a shop boy.

Seger burst out his bedroom door,
whitie-tighties on one half (cowboy hat on the other),
whiskey in one hand (Marlboro in the other).

Maybe Tom's tale was tall, but I doubt it because the story ended with him
asking Bob to have a drink and go bowling.
Sure, Seger said, but stood him up and there was a silence in the truck
and the desert turned that page. I'm sure

if I can build the Adirondack-style bistro set I've promised my wife
for our already-passed anniversary
and the one-by-twos I plan to use for the seats have ass-in-palm perfect
edge routs, I'll be the kind of man Seger wouldn't have stood up,

the kind of man Seger would still be talking about in a Nashville studio.
I'll be the man who ran against the wind and won. A router
used to be a ruffian, a plunderer, a rogue or robber, but

in the right hands a word can round and become
that look, the lovin' I pray for in someone's eyes.

Usable Past

—after Sir Philip Sidney

Restringing the lights on the house
     readying for winter again, when we need
those twinkle-kiss sometimes
     to remind us we're not soul-less.
The new strand sags in the middle—a prepositional
     phrase—I never can wrap around

the corner like the old glass bulbs—
     their size, their weight, like an iamb's—
would hold fast the roof's edge, making the turn.

     Maybe I'm forcing the light strings' meter into form
trying to make too much with too little, maybe
     I don't know how to trust the lines together or apart.
All those light-filled boxes stacked in the attic,
     All those years wound into each other.
My unwrapping, straightening them, every year

     laying out and working through each
to find the bulb gone wrong; my compulsion
     to put up with the lights that no longer light

because my father and grandfather struggled
     through the same lines; because the dark line behind
the new is a second coming, which I believe means
     I'm still trying. Isn't memory the same?
The lights I fight aren't only mine.
     They are my labor for a family gathered,

my epitaph to Christmas, my way
     to invite the world to pause with me,
believe in mysteries written after dark.

'Tis the season for labor and looking,
believing in a magic nobody wants to explain,
        strolling our streets like a new world
we've made in lights, what we've made
        together from our pasts, our faith, that
the wisest scholar of the wight most wise

        By Phoebus' doom, with sugred sentence says
That Vertue, if it once met with our eyes,
        strange flames of love it in our soules would raise.

Permission

Let's take the back roads, my wife says,
      so we can see something beautiful. "Beauty,"
         says Sir Joshua Reynolds, "is for anyone who seeks

a serious road, not just aesthetes." I'm never enough
      over myself enough to see outside the white lines.
         We've got this time together, my wife says, can't we enjoy it?

On the back-roads, we're in a black hole,
      and we could have been there an hour ago. If only. As much
         as I look in the rearview, you'd think I could see myself

the way she sees me. Maybe then I'd understand
      I'm not the complicated man I want to be, believing
         travel's never easy, imagining myself a man ragged

walking on the roadside and a man riding ragged
      in my F-150's comfort, checking the clock, not seeing
         the herd of black bears in my periphery is actually

black angus littering the pastoral hillside.
      I should spend more time reading Chaucer,
         Wordsworth who, along with my wife, see the vernacular

in being where you are, who believe the getting there
      is there. How I have separated travel and traveling.
         At a Midwest nowhere crossroads, I'm laying on the horn,

screaming for an unseen thing to turn
      in front of me. Permission's right of way
         I can't imagine or maybe that I won't.

Vocabulary

Maybe you meant to say, Doctor. Maybe you meant,
Doctor is everything fine? But you said
Father instead. As if there was a father
different than the one in the room, yourself, you

new father standing in a room looking at a new mother.
Maybe you meant to say God. You probably meant
Reverend. He stood in front of the church
where you used to go on Sundays to sing yourself

into the second and third persons. You could see
yourself talking to yourself as if you were some other
body moving its lips to the organ,
another presence in your voice

as if the hymnal's words were directions for the self
you could see yourself addressing.
You once said,
I call you Father, I call you Reverend, I call you

Sacred and Holy—these words nobody can explain,
these words feeling like the greatest hoax,
the most real. It's the both/and that troubles

you, he said. How a person can become a moment,
a father, for instance, and a child. You'll be
standing in a room one minute, just a son. Then,
a plow, a yoke, a row to hoe, like nothing happened.

Anonymous

Because the sun sits on the horizon
I imagine a piano. I hate myself
        because I never took piano lessons. I
                hate that I
        didn't just see you
at the Coke machine, or walking through the front yard
I know you played in once upon a time. Once in
        time. Upon the green
                leaves of grass.
        Because the sun hovers like

        a guitar's note, I believe I can make
something like a symphony because the light, right
        before it leaves the day makes me, for
                one second,
        able to admit
alcoholics do what we can when we can. And
when we can't, we hide behind our eyes. People like
        us cast shadows when
                there's no light.
        I am on the edge of asking you

        if you ever wish you could be the sound
a guitar-string makes the moment the finger leaves.
        I am a man you love to want, love
                to want to
        want, and I'm a man
who wants to say what he wants, a man afraid of wants.
Not for the part about the girl, but for the end.
        There's always a girl.
                There's always
        an end. You told me once you'd be

        the sound a doorstopper makes when it's flicked.
I keep that under my hat. I keep the idea
        of love folded in my wallet, where
                I keep the
        invisible sounds
I've accumulated in the last thirty years. You
said, once, I should sit, write out my misguided head.
        I said I can't fight
                anymore.
        I hate it. It takes me out of

everything. You said, Stop then; that easy.
I know, I said, I know, but I am not an easy man.
   And I hate that about myself. I'm
      forever
   walking a city
in my mind, a cold in the air acting as if
my Members Only jacket's not leather, and I'm
   never looking up
      because I
   would have to leave my head. I am

   forever walking with the knowledge that
someone somewhere is playing the piano I
   never learned to play. In the moments
     when I can
   get over myself,
I can smile, and when I do, I remember once
how I stood in a room lined with strangers and said
   my name. I didn't know
     whether that
   city in my mind had a road

   leading back home, if I had a home.
And I remember thinking I was less concerned
   with concepts than concretes, remember
     feeling that
   difference in trusting
my thoughts and knowing I can enjoy them without
trusting them. The thoughts living in my heart are the
   least dependable
     things I have.
   But this city I walk through, this

   cold in my fingers as I reach for my
cigarettes and lighter, these brown shoes beneath me,
   they'll just be fictions if I can't walk
     in the door,
   take off my jacket,
unwrap my scarf, see home through the heat-turned-water
on my glasses, which I will drink forever if
   I can keep smiling
     when I can't
   understand forgiveness' shape.

Christian Anton Gerard to Scalise from New Orleans

From the airport to my hotel downtown I passed
       these graveyards filled less with stones, but giant stone houses.
       I never get away from the fact I stand above the dead, their

markers are stone hands reaching for my heart,
       and there, and often, I touch those hands
       as I have often upon our meetings because

the hand, the shoulder, the hand on the shoulder's a living gesture,
       a gesture of kinship. Strong—they are the heart's working out—
       but in the cab moving past these New Orleans graveyards,

I can't help but think of cost—The cost of living. The cost of dying.
       Marble and granite's cost.
       Building houses. I've spent much of this morning

rethinking my cost-thoughts. I want to believe they're less for show,
       more for protecting what a family, a breath holds dear, that
       out of the body flies life—Small, a kind of cabin,

a place in the woods on a mountain. Usually
       a house is to me the image of a home,
       as if a home holds our bodies. But then

I think of you in your New York apartment, your love for Loren and tacos,
       your love for those you house in the houses you build
       from pages, from ink—Writing's a thing harder than granite, marble—

where the mind moves like ancient earthcrust bits and seafloor,
       our world's bedrock raised back up into view in the marbling
       that makes marble marble, raised up in the color-specks,

the glittering shatter, the marvel we marvel when pressing our hands
       in prayer. How everything is, was, under pressure. Life's pressure
       will push us one day from our homes. Pressure will

force our families to contemplate where
       our bodies will stay. Pressure
       will force our families and friends to build within

a kind of stone heart that can't burn, turn molten.
       I'm a smoker, an alcoholic, Scalise.
       By all accounts I should go

into the earth before you and everyone else I know.
            A tree has no choice in its becoming timber.
            A tree doesn't know it will fall and turn,

someday, to stone to build the stone houses built
            in, and from, pressure, to house the dead somewhere—
            It occurs to me our living's pressure is knowing

we'll turn into all these things,
            be spread across time. Scalise, this is becoming
            out of hand. I'm out of control—innately and

predisposed to do or be—not by choice, Mike, because I am.
            We didn't choose our births or that we'll die,
            that we met on a mountaintop. I'd even go so far

to say our friendship wasn't a choice—whatever's
            writing us, I think, gives us, though,
            some choice, as two friends in the world.

Early on I thought I was building a house here
            to house our friendship, but that's impossible.
            That metaphor falls apart under pressure—

probably all metaphors do—except
            the living. Next time we meet, let's exchange
            small rocks we've found. Let's swallow the stones knowing

they'll pass through us into toilets somewhere into pipes into
            water somewhere. Let's trust the swallow
            will be stone hearts we give

back to the earth before we go back
            to the earth because we've been
            so lucky to be visible.

To Ansel on His Second Birthday

I should have written you last year. I should've
written three hundred and sixty five words.

It seemed too much for me. It was. My son,
seven hundred and fifty days have happened.

A poem on the occasion of your birthday
is not the place for advice or wishes or hopes,

so years from now when you find this again
in a drawer or some bag filled with papers,

don't be disappointed that I've not said here
those countless things I have for you. I want

you to know I don't know what I will be able
to give, how to imagine what you will make

out of any of this. There are things I know, though.
You are iron-clad-headed and willow-

blossom-hearted. You know how to love.
I don't know if this is a blessing or curse.

For me it is both. For me it depends on the day.
You will feel what others can't imagine.

The way you make *daddy* an iamb sometimes,
a troche others, a spondee when you're on the verge

of dancing. Thank you for verging the verge, erasing it,
for dancing without knowing others ask whether or not to dance.

Maybe this will change. Maybe not. Yet this record remains:
Ansel Christian Gerard, it's a clever innocence

with which you do your sorcery. That's Jackson Browne.
He always makes me feel in love. Love like the iris

you found last week beneath the bushes by the deck.
You nodded as your mother said *purple*.

Do you like purple? You knelt down and took the iris
petals in your hands. You cupped them as one might carry

a baby hedgehog from one hedgehog place to another.
If the pictures and matchbox cars were lost, I'd have that always.

Listen, you have what matters from love, never my whiskey-
oblivioned eyes, never your name slurred out my drunk mouth.

A poem on this occasion, Ansel, can only be to say thank you
for running to instead of from when I come home from work.

Poem with Madrigals

It's a bench in a park where interesting things happen
and a park bench where nothing happens, or
it's a frame of mind. Audre Lorde, Audre Lorde,
rationality is not unnecessary. It serves the chaos
of knowledge. It serves feeling. Ezra Pound, Ezra Pound,
make it new, make it new. The lawn, that crosscut pattern.
I used to say my dad gave the world a haircut
every Saturday, but that's a child's thought, right?
And this is a poem and for some reason I'm not
seeing the meaning behind it all. I'm hearing the birds.
I'm singing their madrigals, thinking of a paper I heard
comparing sixteenth century dance patterns
to sixteenth century poems: Sidney's. Philip Sidney's.
Always with the Philip Sidney. I'm imagining myself old,
rocking in my wife's great grandmother's rocking chair
talking, lecturing the wallpaper on the initial strike in
the voice I heard in *Astrophil & Stella* those years ago
when Rob Stillman stopped time and read out loud
those first few sonnets. My life was changed.
And when I say that out loud I want it to mean something.
I mean, of course, it does for me. One minute
I'd never heard Sir Philip's name. Then I knew.
I don't know what happened then, why I heard it
the way I did. I spent a good two years believing
we shared some DNA or all of it. I found some
relief when they confirmed all humans carry
Neanderthal DNA. I wrote a poem about it
like I do when I think I'm the world's center.
I've spent two bucks on two Cokes and despite our tight budget,
my wife will forgive me the way people in love do who won't
let themselves become the sad characters in fictions we read
over and over as if we know it all.
It's Friday afternoon. I'm looking around.
The birds are still making madrigals, the lines
in the lawn make a parquet dance floor, couples
are holding hands and I'm in love like they are.
Who would want to make this new?

Still Life with Myself Two Years Six Months Sober

Dipped in cold pressed coconut oil, my tongue's
drawing heat in that copper kettle mouth.
Blue smoke's violent flames burn those love-struck lungs.
Hickory-stuffed tinder-box heart. Due south
I face hills spit with fires just like mine.

No moonlight. Those camped in this night want home.
When I tasted my heart I wanted more
to dig rusted language from this tongue's loam.

I tasted war. I stayed in war. Ate
concessions from bones skinned with skin's taut tense.
Cut off the heads and tales from my past's dead weight.
Cooked my tongue's speech to blood–rare present tense.

Take, eat; this is my body given to
me for the remembrance of me in me.

2

Defense of Poetry; or The Poet Explaining Himself

I'd forgotten the moon last night would rise
like most other nights because nights come, dark
and droning on for hours while I'm scared
I've forgotten how to make a sentence or
because the moon's poetry's bright cliché.
When I tell someone I'm a poet
they say, *I don't know anything about poems*—
Take the moon's picture tonight, I should say,
show it to a stranger, ask if they see
grief or grievance, joy. Ask if we sometimes
gamble for the impossible because.

Poetry Can Save The World?

I used to believe that when the world was big as Friday night
in a T-top Camaro doing eighty-five in a forty. Didn't we all

pick up the pen for some vainglory? A hand on a thigh,
a tear on the tongue, because we believed

in immortality? I ran into hell because love is
hell (or a dog from hell if you ask Bukowski).

Beatrice was a moth on a tree's trunk.
If Virgil spoke to me I would've become

a burnt-corpse-barge across the river Styx. I was
different than everyone. I opened doors with only my right hand

because everyone told me Jesus was his father's right hand
and I was right handed so I was Jesus, maybe,

or somebody else worth recording. And everyone
said the famous poets judge this universal life,

deciding what's in and what's out—maybe poems
about poems have become taboo as poets say louder and

louder that poetry can save the world.
I didn't know, *properly attended to, delight, as well as havoc,*

is suggestion, so I didn't know language is choice.
Dear Mary Oliver, you asked if one can *be passionate*

about the just, the ideal, the sublime, and the holy, and yet
commit to no labor in its cause. I think you meant writing.

The labor. *Be ignited, or be gone,* you say. What an ordeal
to imagine eternal fire. Most run from it, straight to prayer.

Prayer is what I do when I don't know, or rather
in a poem it's the way I ask the sky to sing.

Defense of Poetry; or Prayer in Recovery

> Rest in soft peace, and, ask'd, say, "Here doth lie
> Ben Jonson his best piece of poetry."
> –Ben Jonson

Like so many millions of praying mantises, I am
in a doorway, in a near field, in a leaf nest waiting

out the guilt deluge carried in everyone's elbows.
This is not a plea for redemption. This is not

a plea for restitution, though it is a thought moving
toward such a thought. Ben Jonson, I presume

you're familiar with what is, what was, and
what shall be because you said your son was

your best piece of poetry. Father, let
rote memory go astray during vespers. Father,

you're familiar with Ben Jonson—psalms and
poems testified and there's record of his life spared

in 1598 by virtue of literacy. Father, you spared
Ben Jonson because he could read and so plead

benefit of clergy. Benefit to me, a member of the reading
public. Poetry from Poiesis: Making, the act

or process. Fiction: Proceeding from invention
and all the ways men find to try and say that thing.

Help me read a past strewn with what can be
read as coincidence and not-coincidence, what can be

construed as something more than those words placing people
and people in the same space at the same time.

No two things can occupy the same space. Poetry and Fiction.
Ben Jonson's Ben Jonson. What is your son, Ben Jonson?

A fiction or a making? A process? So many hours of my life
are indented in church pew-backs, asking and asking

for a clean slate, for perfect words in perfect prayer.
My son, please Father, let me watch his tiny hands work

through the air, hear exhaustion's exuberant moans.
Hold my son close. What I can't imagine and never stop.

Defense of Poetry; or Alcoholic Expected Home

Christmas, again, and Mother, you're weeping
      like the Madonna in story, paint, concrete and marble,
          whatever else artists' hands make weep

in the faithful's hearts. The mother is always left.
      Such is the story of sons trading womb for womb for womb.
          But the Virgin's stories aren't chiding the son

for spending a holiday—in part—with a higher power.
      Sons are born by leaving, Mother. You've known this.
          I have stayed a boy after years drinking, through girls

and women and laying down so they could walk on me.
      You named me for a man I've never known
          who was my grandfather who was named for Christ

and strictly speaking, this conversation about where
      and how exactly and when exactly I'll arrive home
          to celebrate my December birth feels less like mass

and more like I'm holding Dante's hand after he's installed
      an escalator in hell for those who need to get there quick.
          When in August you asked about my Christmas plans

I opened first a beer, then the whiskey making my devil sing.
      I sang songs I pray my mouth won't sing again.
          Symphosius' twelfth riddle says: *There's an earthly*

house which sounds with a clear note, a tone,
      and the house itself makes music but contains
          a silent guest and both hurry onward, guest and house

together—Mother, I hurried past my past. I left
      without saying my silence. I returned to tell
          my story. I've been a guest in my house, yours.

I used to call you drunk to prove I wasn't, think
      you couldn't hear my slurred name. Your
          worry's been a music calling me rightly to myself.

Ars Poetica

I've been sulking around the house

wringing my hands inside my chest
like some old weatherman

certain the big storm's coming today,

the one that'll blow us all away
with whatever wrath you believe in.

If you ask me how I am, I'll tell you

my recent life's story, which is ridiculous.
Yesterday, for instance, I found a dead mole

in the driveway. Nice job, cat, I thought, then

remembered the star-nosed mole I caught
years ago. I put the mole in the plastic aquarium

I'd used to kill a Siamese fighting fish.

I gave the mole grass and leaves, some twigs
and watched him for two days. I named him

Frightful. I never saw him move,

except his little ribs heaving like a coal miner's.
I pressed my face to the plastic, staring

into those mineshaft eyes. I was sure

he was scared of me, but I don't remember
if I felt like God or like I thought God might feel.

What's carried in my chest's never my choosing,

so the stories I tell are always the same,
why my prayers keep begging for words

to let me re-write my own endings, or

at least imagine the possibility, a sunrise
on the horizon I can't see in the dark.

I remember the body, though,

after I'd stared him to death,
how it bounced in the grass on the third day.

I remembered yesterday when I flicked that mole

with my shoe's tip into the road, the traffic
like a life-full of guilt.

Water Skiing with Robert Creeley

I hold various headshots I've cut from my own photographs over your face
just to feel the wind blowing a few of your curls,
that little outboard's vibration under your hand on that lake
(at least I imagine it a lake) when I take your *Selected Poems* off the shelf.

Isn't power a weird thing? The boat's wake suggests some decent speed.
Sometimes I imagine if you sneezed right as Bruce Jackson snapped that photo
and your head bent down, I'd be back there in the middle of the wake
slalom skiing, waving one hand in the air.

People would wonder if I was waving at the camera or to you and Bruce.
Maybe I'd be about to put a thumb up or down as if to say speed on or slow now.
The water's rougher than it looks but nobody can tell because
Robert Creeley's driving a boat, having his picture taken, and probably writing

a poem in his head or at least thinking to himself, This will become
a poem. I mean, really, how often does anyone drive
a boat without looking, while posing and pulling a skier?
I'm sorry that I'm writing this to you in a present that is and isn't yours.

But I wasn't smart enough to know you before now. I'm still not, but Art Smith was
smart enough to tell me to buy your poems because he knew they would be good for me.
Like William Carlos Williams saying, *there, and there* to you
because *what one wants is / what one wants, yet complexly* as you say he said.

When I read your poems, especially the early ones, I feel like I'm skiing behind you
into a whale's mouth. What a stunt it is to live, you say, when I climb into the tiny boat.
You pat my back, hand me a pen, paper, and bottle. Nobody'll believe us about this whale,
you say, And the paper's not waterproof, but trust will get it where it needs to go.

Defense of Poetry; or Love Prayer Prayed by Christian Anton Gerard

I've known and forgotten Newton, maybe,
I don't know, anticipation and reaction, feeling
without and fulfilled, how I can think of sitting
next to you at room temperature and I'm not cold,
but the quiche feels frigid in the same air, the same mouth.
We're always saying we'll make time for each other,
and I'm so thankful you put on that green thing I love
to love you in like all the rainforests' leaves pouring their hold
over me. The quiche over there's almost got me upset.
My hunger. Its quiet consternation. Sometimes
I want to claim even my books are against me
rather than admit I'm lonely up here in the kitchen
while you're down with the sleepless baby,
all green with life. I don't think it'd be out of line
to say a little prayer that when he's off and dreaming
we'll be green with living, our bones green embers,
neither of us giving a damn about the quiche, which is
on the stove cooling, turning, our room-temperature love
when we're most hungry—something about the physics of it
all. A fallen apple. An eaten apple. Or another theorem.

Defense of Poetry

In the time I've read and lost Rilke's *Book of Images*,
generations of ants have come and gone, the river-

birch planted last year, grown shaggy like a teenaged boy
in his old man's eyes. Get a job, mine used to say, Get a wife

and don't lie to her about anything. You're lucky enough
if she wants to marry you. Don't think your luck'll get any better.

I remember being in the same shoes as every kid wondering how
we'd know we're grown up. I remember the nail going through

the sole of my foot and Kangaroo shoe, the good burn—
peroxide taking tetanus away. I remember looking

at the hardened, pretty adults, wanting their value, seeming rarity.
Oysters make pearls because sand scares them.

If the world is my oyster, what is my pearl?
My wife is pregnant so I've been thinking

what a son or daughter should know first about the world.
I become worried I don't mean the world. Really,

I mean what a son or daughter should know about me,
what I think is the world. That there's so little

time scares me the most. Since I read and lost Rilke's
Book of Images, I keep thinking of that one line in the middle

of that poem in the middle: *as the evening unbuttons its blouse.*
My God. I wish I could tell you the title. For the life of me.

What an image to be made in—as if an evening were someone
wearing a blouse, as if an evening could be worn like a life.

Christian Anton Gerard Thinking He's Milton's Adam

I can't be the only one waking up
thinking I'm Adam looking down at my
hand in Eve's, clouds rumbling, the Miltonic

narrator: *The world was all before them.*
I can't be the only one scared shitless
imagining that first night outside

the garden. I've imagined paradise
atop a grassy hill taller than all,
the way Red Cross Knight sees that bright city

on the hill, and I've imagined always
the world outside just as lush as inside
and Adam and Eve hand in hand atop

history's tallest hill looking out across
the forests and fields below thinking
they'd lost something despite having

gained the whole rest of the world. Imagine
what they must have thought looking up, seeing
the fallen sky for that first time? Broken?

What could Adam have thought of those night lights
without Milton's narrator telling him
what to think? How can a man muster a wish

out loud, or not, when his maker's made himself known?
Cast him out? I can't be the only one who's been
out in the night, two hands opened screaming,

"if I can't make it with my own hands,
if the lean-to leans to the ground, and
the Solomon Seal's all I know to eat,

I'll make it if this world's a wilderness
with room for those who'll give themselves to it."
Maker, don't let me be the only alcoholic

who stands out under your stars praying
all the lights I see are others who've lived
by listening to all the words you've made.

Sublime Prayer for an Alcoholic

Christian Anton Gerard, Duende
calls you to sea or to stand
for a stranger's honor. Duende
reaches inside, grabs below
the heart, deeper, deep
in the self you don't know
you have. Duende
takes its time, reaches so deep
with fingers closing into a fist
grabbing pulling out
what it took
so long to reach, to know. Pain
so great your legs fall away,
your torso's there floating in fear
praying out loud for Duende,
below your heart, for Duende
to pull you through cunning
streets, graveled self, a gallows
where every hanging skeleton
gives one bone and one bone only
for Duende. Take from your past
one bone from inside your head.
Christian, pray inconsolably.
If you could only stand in one place
on your own legs, feel grass, or rocks,
thorns, dead leaves. If your mouth
and legs could be in the same place.
Dear Duende, singing peace—
Christian's body quiet, the mountain
he's imagined standing afront
for years. Those sheer,
ancient faces inside waiting.
Dear Duende, help him collapse.

Confession of the Alcoholic Poet Who Brought Books into a Public Restroom

I've rung deep red bells for so long now
        I don't know anymore if hands are knots
        or if I'm hanging on by choice. I've been
        wanting a pen fast as my heart
        in those nine-alarm moments. I keep reading
        all these poems about poems and poets
        trying to become what I read, as if
        I'm convinced that's how a real poem's made.
Everything in this life happens so fast.

Even my shits come on like wildfire and
        next I know I'm in the workshop checking
        that wood-glue joint I clamped last night
        trying to say out loud all the poets' names I know
        so I can know I know enough. Honestly,
        I've been trying for years to get a shit
        into a poem because Liam Rector's
        "I Get a Feeling" showed me how to turn
a phrase, but "I Get a Feeling" is about poems,

becoming okay with this life. Today
        I opened Gerald Stern's *Paradise Poems*
        thinking I'd try a different perspective
        on paradise, and there's Stern writing his
        "In Memory of W.H. Auden,"
        turning some bum sleeping on street grilles
        in New York City into Ovid and himself.
        Gerald, you know so much about Ovid,
your poem makes me feel like I'm just trying.

For shit's sake, look at me, this pity party
        because I might be poetry's asshole.
        Because I can't tell if I'm more or less
        connected to you, Gerald, because once
        I saw a Bleeker Street sign in New York,
        or because I say over and over
        I know that I don't know
        enough to see Ovid's incarnation
on the street, like you, which is why your poem's

a Paradise Poem and mine's still obsessed
       with shit. Remember when you wrote *Ovid's*
       become his own sad poem? How did you know?
       It's happening to me right now, isn't it?
       How did you not become your own sad poem?
       Is that paradise? Is there any way to know,
       but to keep imagining it's beyond this poem
into the next, like the best toilet-stall graffiti?

Gerald, were you comfortable
       sitting between Rome and New York, ancient
       and modern, all the noises? Did you know
       Liam Rector? Did you *get a feeling*
       of discomfort, pressure? Did you *feel that*
       pressure to be a good person? Poet?
       Did you *wait for the feeling*
       and then when it [did come] do its bidding?
Or, like him, *on a very good day,*

did you *not much give a shit about that?*
       I'm in a toilet-stall trying to follow
       the scrawled connected voices, but
       I can't stand up, burst into the next
       stall to see where the conversation goes.
       I'm stuck here, crouched between knowing
       and not, between urges making me
       animal, and this feeling,
this human pressure.

[You've seen him looking up from the table]

or over his shoulders. His table is clean.

His menu's wearing at the creases, a pair of jeans
pulled on then off again, like lies or insomnia.

Probably you realized he walked in
because he's already hungry, not to sit and become

hungry. Why not stroll in, sit down, declare,
Nothing now, thank you, like an aura,

*I'm going to work up a craving for something
while I check out this literature?* He'll open

the menu. Why not mull it over, like an aura,
mull over everyone in the place?

He looks familiar, like the deer you almost felled
last winter in the woods, the deer you held

in your crosshairs, couldn't shoot because
the trees were ripe with bark. A deer need

not make a decision. Don't overthink it, you
said to yourself. A deer knows what it wants

when it walks into the dusk. What did you want
when you walked in here? You're staring

at yourself in the horizon. What do you want?
Maybe you should offer yourself a beer. Maybe

you should flip yourself the bird. You could,
though, look straight into your eyes, recite Mark Strand's

"Breath" again for the thousandth time because you're alone
and that poem *stands on one leg while the other one dreams,*

because that poem's a clouded bed of concrete chips.
You could say "Breath" straight into your eyes, the window's

night-shine, a million headlights gone
through your bloodstream, your hummingbird heart.

You've waited long enough and now you need.

Blood Is No More Life than a Cloud Resembling a Goose Is a Goose

Winter-time's when I pull the dead

grass from the garden bed because the spiders sleep

or have moved to other haunting grounds

in my mind as I sit down in the dirt

and the mint leaves come off their stalks

inch by inch while I pull the dead from the earth.

How often I've wandered into gardens or woods

and thought how near to nature I am. How often

I have sat watching a clover grow with the same attention

I give to confessing my obsessive compulsion

near the knife-block, as I imagine pulling my own dead

from myself. How it would look, the paring knife stuck

in my thigh, the warm blood tricking me into calling it life.

Come now. My fingerprint ridges are filled with

whatever makes mint smell like mint. What a condition.

Hands that have damaged. Hands unafraid, ripping clover

from the ground. Hands delighting in the discord

struck by the bee's sting as it crawls from underneath

a clover's leaves. I sat to weed, to make this garden

a thing more beautiful than nature could have made.

I sat striving for what should be and could be, but

the tiny bee, its stinger in my green thumb, its body

writhing, burying itself before me reminds me

my making a golden world means accepting the fallen

world, where I live. If this garden is my trying to make

another nature, then I must delight in my dumb thumb,

the pain that happens, when though I pray,

I mistake my sounds of penance for forgiveness.

Pastoral Instinct of a Recovered Alcoholic

I've been eating her Midol this morning
        since I bent to pick up a hickory scrap
to practice routing on the new router

        I ran out and bought after receiving
the rotary tool router attachment I sent away for
        by mail, which I received, then burnt up the tool,

which induced the kind of panic a man panics
        when he's alone in the workshop—a man
and his tools and her birthday's tomorrow.

        Of course I looked at the wood scraps,
the picture-frame pieces I'd already mitered
        and thought, What the hell? Why not blow her mind

and lay a bell-shaped rout on these edges,
        so it looks like I know what I'm doing?
Can "rout" be a noun and not mean "to fight"?

        The OED says "a sharp sudden pull; a jerk,"
"a bellow or lowing sound, as of cattle," and
        "a loud noise, especially of the sea, thunder, etc…"

I felt all these in bending
        for the hickory scrap
when my back decided I should imagine

        what a wolf's teeth might feel like if I stray
too far in my thoughts, believe I'm able
        to believe I can make what I want when I want.

I was proud of using rout as a noun in a thought.
        A recovered alki's s'posed to be patient with thoughts.
Impatience is a wolf in the pasture at night.

        I'm lying on the floor, a newborn calf. How
can I stand, run without panic, keep
        hungry what walks the night.

A Knife's Signature in His Alcoholic Palms

He didn't know why his glassblower worked in steel
until she explained the move from solid to molten to skin-thin
to the crucially over-tangible point

when even he could melt. When he walks into her apartment
and she tries to apologize about calling again, she means she loves
how a body solders without heat and he must admit

what he's cut from himself to make himself
a wrought iron table, where his other editions come for beer
and whiskey's bite, then erase.
Of course they'd met in a bar where he worked. Of course they drank

their hands together. This is, after all, a story worried
about getting it right. He moltens of his own accord, is kicked out of her accord,
so he steals her groceries—

thin-sliced peppered turkey, one time deviled eggs, sometimes bread, bananas,
and marmalade, but never, ever, her admission that she could try
a medium between glass and steel.

Skin, he says, starts the switchbacks
toward the devil's door and he can't fit
that fact out the window

and whoever she was or is or turns into in her whiskey mirror.
Each is a thief seen in the blown-steel heart she's made
and when she holds it up for him to see, he sees

his blown-steel heart is a mold hollowed
like the space between one and one.
He told her once of his earlier editions, the drinking with them

over himself—the girl who found
a knife's signature in his alcoholic edition's palm,
when Lucifer found a little leather square depicting Lucrece's rape

in blood with his face stitched over Lucrece's
in the stomach of an edition whose teeth were busted out.
Why Lucrece? she asked. Why do you live yourself into fables?

What next? Will you believe an edition of you is jumping over the moon?
Lucrece, he said, isn't a fable. It's a story about the self's breakability.
This is why she can't make him her medium, why she made
his blown-steel heart—

so she could say his face is why she couldn't stop
letting him have himself to himself.
This is to say what we agreed up front we'd never learn to say, that
I remember steel and glass, paper and skin are unrelenting accidents.

Pastoral: Can We Say Cowboy Anymore?

It is now illegal to herd sheep
through the canyons. How then
are we to read America's story?

What will become of the strong silent
cowboy? I've made camp half way up

a nameless mountain. Tomorrow I will
see the fifteen sheep I purchased
from a southwest Virginian.

I will heard them to my home
in east Tennessee. I'm an outlaw without a gun.

My world's unsnapping its pearl-snap.
Samuel Daniel was right. The wise are above books.
It is for the General sort that we write.

The man who owned my sheep kept a large white farmhouse
clad in a black roof's armor.

He said white cools in summer, black heats in winter,
and he lives accordingly up or down
in the house in which I saw no books.

Now that I walk with sheep, I feel the wolves' circle
though he said none are here. I feel the black bear's

taste for flesh, though he said bears are afraid of man.
I've bought black electrical tape and have crossed out
the "cowboy" printed on my pearl-snap.

I walk back to Tennessee a general sort of man
believing the cowboy man I left yesterday

wise and above what I am doing here.
I'd thought these letters would find you
somewhere after I had returned with my flock,

after I had taken them to market or wherever
they're supposed to go. I'd thought this waterproof

paper would be the key, surviving my story into what
I cannot imagine. But for safekeeping I will
print these words on the skins I've skinned and

tanned. This will be my legacy, my way
to bring the America's story back into view. Or, rather,

my story is not the words on the skins of the sheep
who have helped me outlaw in a time without outlaws
but the skins themselves, which you hold in your hands.

Defense of Poetry; or Poem with Bowling Leagues and Black Dresses

Give me driving in a tiny green car and
a six string acoustic strummed to damage.
Give me a lip bitten despite the dark and

the way a streetlight insinuates safety.
Give me the waiting while the black dress
is traded for another black dress and

then another black dress before jeans and
a sweater will be what is worn on the walk
to the bowling alley near the street's end.

I'll take hours talking
about the romantic nature of bowling leagues.
Give me a humpback whale breathing in

the dusk and the dawn below the cliffs
where three million puffins are making love.
Account now for the crying at a wedding and

the crying it takes to sleep through the heart's
hardest hurricanes that seem never to have an eye.
There is the voice in the shower and the car and

there is the voice on the phone and across counters,
tables, dance floors, open fields and campsites.
Give me the fire that's hardest to start and

the breath kindling the stories told and retold.
Say over and over the scientific names of passion-
flowers, iris and tulips, succulents I have to touch

because they are Earth's connection to outer space.
Give me every language in the world,
every word of every language in the world,

but don't, if there is one, give me a word meaning
the way you are my orange-purple infinite mystery.
Such a word, darling, would give me, what

I've given my life to never figure out.

Poet Seeing Stars

—for Stephen Christian Gerard and Christian Ezra Gerard

It was night. Down
the beach, a fire

throwing auras
to air, auras

as Plato saw
outside his own cave

looking up, not in.
Christian Anton Gerard

thought the scene
a universe inside a universe

like a freighter,
with portholes. Hushed,

the surf-siren's
voice, a red tide.

The night, a room
without a roof without

walls without electric
lights. The story of

Christian's grandfather's
right-hand man who

one Monday, said he'd
re-roofed his house, how

he couldn't sleep though,
the roof blocked the stars

he used to watch before
sleep. How that man could

see night in night,
his shadow in stars.

Or Dear John Ashbery,

Maybe it's nothing
more than heat, humidity rolling
like a great chariot across the land,

Midwestern, either hills or flat, patched
with trees and fences. There's the
willow we climbed as boys, our neighborhood,

a canvas on which emerges a chorus of smiles.
A winter morning, copied almost with
carbon from a Highlights page

where kids stuff themselves in snowsuits and run
through the water flakes that look like paper,
taste like whatever colored mitten yarn.

There's the oak bonfire smoke, the dry, young night
lit up with northern lights, tendrils,
joined as though speech, ferns fiddleheading out

of my stratosphere's wild, inky eye. Maybe
a weather no one can forecast.
Every time I read "Some Trees," I think how big

a poem can be on a single page, how many
years I walked outside, said, Trees,
are you trying to tell me I am anything?

Am I hoping there's more than ambient light
I conjure because it's missing, or so I've thought?
The wind doesn't wind through itself.

Dear John, I make.
Anything forecastable is what I bring
to this grove of trees I don't believe a forest proper.

Your poem where I'm a man ill-equipped
to face myself, my weather, your poem
where the stars aren't out, but the world is.

Defense of Poetry; or Poem in Which I Can't Imagine My Own Death
—for Marilyn Kallet, who is right

For years I've looked to those newly abandoned
sons, like Ed Hirsch and Mark Halliday so I could cry

for my own father who is still living.
Something about the deadness of a dead father.

All the questions I'll need to ask the second I can't.
Mark and Ed are sons and fathers. And now I'm a father

hearing their voices. *Give me back my father walking the halls,*
Ed cries, and *Everybody's father dies; but* / Mark admits

when my father died it was my father. Now I'll be
the dead father. My son doesn't know

yet. I've begun reading everything I can about imagination
so I can prove I'll never leave if he can imagine me,

which means I'm learning how to reimagine everything.
I keep saying Jill Rosser's: *I wonder* / *why I ever wanted to read*

a book, / *such a time-* / *consuming life draining impediment,*
precisely / *what I feared she'd be when I allowed myself* /

to admit I feared her, before she showed her face.
For years I've been trying to say poetry's power

with living's business. Marilyn Kallet said, Relax,
you'll find a way to do what you have to. Something

will change—your writing will deepen.
I didn't know how to believe her then.

How can I face myself and grieve my living father? How
can I look at my son and not imagine him grieving me?

I used to be fine with my own mortality. Parenting, it
makes the old ego a new frame of mind, a picture picturing

what's felt when the heart wants nothing else
but to change how it once felt. I stood that night,

heard Marilyn, and my ego stared me down.
You're too selfish to father, my ego said, and look,

you're so selfish you've imagined me floating above you,
like one of Plato's ideal yous. You can't hide from me.

And I won't lie. You're so good at being selfish
you can't imagine your own death,

being the dead father, leaving your son a life's worth of
questions he doesn't know how to ask.

If I were you, I'd start asking why you're waiting for your death
to start saying the words a father never knows to say.

Aubade in Afternoon

We should take a shot
of cognac, a walk. Some
days I believe desire

is its own penance. Some
days, I know if I would have
done that, it would have come

out looking like a bird. Some
times I bite the pill in half
that calms me. Sometimes

the biting makes me calm.
I am a tornado in its own eye.
Sometimes I think the world

waking upsets twilight, and
sometimes it feels more like
the sky's a giant sequoia seed

cracking from the moon's heat.
Nice alliteration, you say.
But if it be syntax inverted

you love, let me
be that wrangling, that
reverse sentence full—

your boots on still jeans
my hands reach slide
listen let us be denim

its working to the floor
the sound of.

Christian Anton Gerard Is Unable To Be Opaque

I'm kind of a Swayze aficionado.
I've seen Roadhouse and Dirty Dancing.

I've seen Ghost. I've cried because I'm a man.
I've always confused opaque with obsidian.

I once held a stone to the sun
as if the stone held secrets like her

blended eye-shadow, the shades of grey,
a classy elevator's insides. Hold the door.

Hold that blink for one second longer.
The stone is a vessel.

Her eyes—something else entirely.
If an object is a memory system,

then her eyes cannot be objects,
windows for instance, as in

eyes are windows to the soul; what a crock.
Windows have crappy backstories.

Windows are for making space.
Eyes are not for making space.

Opaque pupils. Opaque desire, which
Swayze couldn't keep opaque because he smiled.

Smiles are like eyes.
Describing smiles is something poets do.

And you're a woman who smiles
so you're indescribable. Maybe

when I say hello you'll think of the tradition—
poets describing smiles and we can just go on

without pretense, unabashed.
Try and say night's not a tincan phone.

Do you hear the tin can ringing?
What stays in my ear is an orange tree in fall.

What stays in yours? It is how I want to talk,
that tree I told you of, all orange and raining leaves.

Holdfast: My Alcoholic Head in Recovery
—after Yehuda Amichai

Sometimes there's no room for the third person.

Sometimes I think of artifice as if

my hummingbird heart can't hum or slow,

so I set down my thoughts on a twig

and say *I am not I* over and over

until I'm more comfortable with not being I

so I can hide something in the third person.

I sat in the stacks imagining every voice in every book

on every shelf saying themselves out loud at the same time.

That's how I imagine infinity and loneliness.

New York City at rush hour, Paris or Berlin.

I want so badly to separate them all out

and listen perfectly so I don't have to be

a voice a part of anything, so rather than the third person

there will be only a guitar's sound in the night,

not strumming, but picking out each note

in Moonlight Sonata, like a single leaf off

the willow I used to climb, reaching for a single wisp

of night. Behind all this some great happiness is

hiding. And still, most nights, I sit in the dark,

knees drawn to my chest and all the words I know

dangle like ghosts I can't grip, can't stop gripping.

Tonight the Space You Need

Bats out tonight.
Reaching as I used to
for the past when thirty
beers couldn't quiet
my chest's demons.
I'm hard pressed for quiet.
I say mercy tonight.
Fire means anything.
Bats though. The moon.
Are what they are. Life
on life's terms. I pray
orange coursing
in what you left
to come to me
to make this life we
watched catch like
the skids I lit tonight.
Fire's not consistent,
takes and takes and is
an alcoholic in it hard.
I pray you're well out there.
Moon's gotta be somewhere
throwing the fickle sun's
colors on what I can't see
but somehow feel. Tonight
I don't want anything
in your way. Quiet
presses hard when
a man like me wants
to hold a woman like you
through bats, moons, fires
that are what they are
because they were.
I say mercy tonight.
I say tonight is tonight.
Hell will still be
full in the morning.

Christian Anton Gerard, a Shearsman of Sorts
—after Wallace Stevens

Christian Anton Gerard's trying
    to pin down a self, trying to understand
        self in a whole's context. The man

with the blue guitar knows things
    as they are are changed upon
        the blue guitar. Stevens knew

a self's world breathes imagination.
    Christian Anton Gerard didn't know
        sometimes the world breathes us as we are,

changed in a poem, so he imagines himself surprised
    by death, imagines the poet's billowing breath, imagines
        senses like night's coming, sleep's deep need. The poem

collects senses and imagines breath's terrifying bellows to show
    Christian Anton Gerard his life, an old man before a fireplace,
        singing a blue guitar's song, what he needs to close his eyes.

Sobering Interrogative: A Man's Most Vulnerable

when in his pockets he carries want and need and
in his chest and heart his lungs he carries

want and need when he comes upon a place
where a decision must be made I imagine

the place a forest clearing at dusk
In the moment before dark I see colors truest

I trust that I trust I'm at terms with terms
My son will never be apart from me even if

there's distance between us I know I can trust
a woman, her, trust she has all my ribs and

that I'm better in making vulnerable my heart
It deserves to beat All hearts do but some hearts

can't hear their own kairotic beat That's not our tale
Thank the Muses I've carried Steven Dunn's line

Let love when it can be a form of containment
on my tongue because I want those words true

Such are lovers' existential thoughts
Love says you will die to lovers

because lovers want love to be past death
We can imagine everything else is paper we make

when in us we see nature's objects and objections
She is not punctuation She is a font

If I was told I could write one name Hers
or my wife's I would stand The nail in my hand

I would carve hers I would build her a swing

Christian Anton Gerard Reads Her

—after Her and thinking of Bob Dylan reading at Chloe Kiel and
Ray Gooch's place circa '61 or '62

There's no lettering, just filigreed
lips binding the covers of
the books of the girl
                with books for eyes and the filigree
delicate as mascara
applied with care makes

her unread books what Christian carries
like eyes in his mind's knapsack
as he hops freight train
                after freight train into the night. And
when the moon sits just so, his
pulse's voice says, "trust

more than silence is made by her pale
electricity." Hours
only matter when
                counted. Silence is a learned skill,
like how to find pleasure in
squeezing a lit fire—

work into his night's tight fist. Christian
is counting. How the minutes
account for seven
                cookies, thirty picked up pine cones. An
afternoon. A morning. The
time it takes to add

the hours, to hold everything held
in a poet's cracked voice,
pleasure in the wind's
                quiet, her skirt's hem brushing her legs.
There's something quite romantic
about the dryer steam

passing in front of the window while
February thaws his hard-slept heart.
Christian prays to her,
                his breath in front of him like words
he wishes she could hear him
say to her. Don't sleep

dear girl with books for eyes, Christian prays,
tell me of looming years, how
to breathe in each tense.
                    Christian Anton Gerard's lying, the dark
and her and him in his mind,
against an almost—like Dylan's harmonica

hanging on his neck—orange tree in a minor chord. And her,
she's covering Lovesong by
The Cure by breathing.
                    There's no lettering, just filigreed
lips binding the covers of
the books of the girl

with books for eyes and the filigree
delicate as mascara
applied with care makes
                    her unread books what Christian carries
like eyes in his mind's nap sack
as he hops freight train

after freight train into his night. And
Christian's not a patient man
etherized on a
                    table. Love's no place a wand'ring face
should reach. No time left for sleep—
She has books for eyes

and Christian's the poem he wants to give
to this woman with books for eyes,
this woman who knows
                    how to wear lipstick when she wears it,
who'd be lying if she said
she didn't know how

to give goosebumps or a kiss, who'd be
lying if she said she didn't
listen to some songs
                    just to hear her heart beat. Christian thinks
of his hummingbird heart: beat,
keep beating because

there's nothing else. No words he may say
despite the delicious sharp
need, which is to read.

Christian Anton Gerard Moving Toward Psalm

—and palm to palm is holy palmers' kiss

How can a prayer move forward in a world turning
        in circles? But the world isn't only
        turning in circles. It moves also
        in elliptical orbit, lilts to one side,

Christian Anton Gerard holding a prayer
        book, the weight of psalms at rest. The world
        circles he supposes in so many circles—
        the universe in space, eye's iris in evening.

Maybe Christian Anton Gerard's the earth and
        the bodies he knows are other planets,
        the sun like a year in a psalm. Christian
        Anton Gerard believes all narratives move

like the earth and believes the sun's a story
        constantly telling itself slant. Christian Anton
        Gerard needs to look toward the sun, not at.
        He does! Oh goodness. Goodness.

There's tension in joy; a double-bass's string
        snapped taut against the neck, lips in prayer,
        perfect joy and perfect ache for joy and
        doesn't exaltation find us in a field rimmed

by dark as story for story our lovers' hands
        move together telling the one thing that is
        everything? Oh world without end! Oh
        world in the heart's adrenaline-filled-atrium!

Christian Anton Gerard would write
        murder ballads where nobody really dies.
        Christian Anton would write letters to strings
        on certain songwriters' guitars and send them.

He would write himself reminders to have fun,
        to write to get where he needs. The impulse to
        story is a thing one should consider when considering
        one's life, which is one's own, which is often not

said to people like Christian Anton Gerard
        to whom it should have been said,
        Everything is story. Everything.

Defense of Poetry; or The Alcoholic's Imitation

—after Joshua Reynolds' *Discourses on Art*

The greatest natural genius cannot subsist on its own stock;
he who resolves never to ransack any mind but his own

will soon be reduced, from mere bareness, to the poorest
of all imitations. Christian's a genius at choosing wrong

at the exact wrong time. The charge is not to imitate desire.
Christian is an alcoholic. Alcohol's a mystery unsolvable.

Christian's desire's no imitation of a body wanting to seize.
Christian's friend says *problem* is problematic.

Christian's known a world of knives. Screaming skin.
Is a problem a problem if it can't be solved?

Pain and not-pain is a problem. Christian's
slept inside thirty-packs and whiskey handles,

let knives be lullabies in his veins. A problem is pain
and wanting not-pain. Alcohol's desire when in him.

Defense Prayer

—after Adrienne Rich and Sir Philip Sidney

Maker, I've been thinking of poems
as riddles. The voices you've made

whisper a map. I pray for
a cartography through the silences,

through the question "How do I exist?"
If there's a poetry where this could happen

let me listen in all directions. If
there's a poetry where this could happen

bring its writers to me, not as blank spaces,
but words stretched like skin

over meanings, but as silence falls
at the end of a night through which two people

have talked till dawn, have said, Let verse be
verse. Let's let what's said make sense,

let what's said be our poetry's defense.
Muse, say, *fool, look in thy heart and write.*

3

Enargeia

A lace blouse and her
hip-limning paper skirt.
Dressing's enough to know
the body craves touch
one way or another—how
a moment reveals itself.
She was once marionette,
once a dictator. She wanted
seamstress fingers, blues
voice. Point. Counterpoint.
This whole evening—
not a hand to mouth, but
a hanging paper lantern.
And then the wind.

Christian Anton Gerard and Her Yet without a Past

She puts on Cyndi Lauper to be the smokes
they'd smoke if the store wasn't two blocks too far
to walk in the dark. Something about the way

Cyndi makes boys wanna have when she says
girls wanna have fun reminds Christian Anton Gerard
Europeans love Levi's. Or maybe it's her jeans' tag
next to his head when their pockets wear
through weathered years.

In a café yesterday, they overheard an older couple.
The gentleman said something about life's book.
I hate that metaphor, Christian said, that way
I'm never a book.

Tell me, his girl said, how we met.
You knew what you were doing, Christian said,
when you put on that paper skirt.
I watched you read. Your red poems. And you
read my mind when you said I looked like I needed
words in me. We happened

to be seeing other people who weren't
in the room and hours happened
to make us red with life. Quick as that.
Just us yet without a past. And here we sit.

See, she said, a story with an arc,
anything a book can imagine.

It's as if Christian's hopped a plane so he could
jump above her house, parachute into her
room. His tongue to her ears. His breath

in her hair. Her nails,
ten scalpels singing through his skin,
prayers inside a night making each from each.

Her and Christian Anton Gerard in an Argon Cloud

I'm always telling myself, remember your heart's
a muscle the mind's made a metaphor
for every felt thing. There's argon for that

moment—all electrode and flux and steel.
The welding mask's dark glass is what cries
during the cutting of raw onions—that glass

between the eye and the arc. There's a way
to meld so there is one metal. There's a how
to make it seem so. The only way to see

the sun's unflinching, to see it burned in your eye.
Look and blink and look. I'm saying it's the same,
me in love, if you're willing to lift the welding mask's

glass so action and reaction are light. You listen to me
speak in circles. Seeming is less than adequate for the heart.
Seaming, though, a different story. Sometimes I cry

thinking of the way you listen.
Every onion I've peeled is onion at its core.
I don't want to be onion to my core. I want to be

a thing become another thing. Speak of me
in the possessive. Let's look right at us,
for each other. Let us risk our sight.

Defense of Poetry; or How To Say the Heart's Epitome

Don't you love
  thinking of Milton saying inside

and out loud *Paradise Lost?*
  Which was the fire's kindling?

The inner voice?
  The uttered words?

Man's first disobedience?
  The fruit? When Adam & Eve,

hand in hand with wand'ring
  steps and slow, through Eden

took their solitary way, maybe
  the lake's where four streams

murmur fallen water, where
  the fringed bank is with myrtle crowned,

Eve's crystal mirror? She and Milton saw
  in water her virginity,

which was herself—creation
  manifest in man and woman.

Lakes hold liquid, are. Oceans,
  we say, are the epitome of lakes.

Maybe it's like thinking love's
  molten, the lovers making

volcanoes. We say we know
  by difference—something is

by what it's not, but Satan's
  liquid fire lake and Eve's mirror

do what lakes do, hold
            themselves still and awful—

the seconds after two lovers'
            first love, when with eyes wide open

in the dark, you believe you are
            seeing a changed you or

her or him or the world. A lake
            is an ocean is a volcano, is

a fiction. You've become
            more than a body of water.

If you could see inside your lover's
            head, you'd describe lava

rivers flowing, then pooling
            in synapse after synapse.

Giving everything to start again,
            you'd hear the new world's hiss

against the shoreline
            and some miles under

the world's not orange. Its red
            fires aren't looking to go out.

You Poem You

There's this airplane and it's flying. We're probably doing five,
six hundred miles an hour and I just finished reading

a favorite story by Steve Almond. It makes me want to cry
and make love with her who loves me at the same time.

I don't hear enough about men crying, certainly not
while making love. The whole thing's become taboo,

or maybe it always was. I imagine
Tom Hanks in *Sleepless in Seattle* cried

when he and Meg Ryan made love—same thoughts on
Brendan Frasier in *With Honors* and Cusack in *High Fidelity*.

I keep looking at the clouds, remembering looking at the clouds
when I was a kid, my first time on a plane. How my hands were

jumping beans, how I kept checking on the jumping beans
to make sure they were still jumping— proof of life.

I didn't want them to die.
They were in my pocket on that plane and the clouds were

there. So fast. Five, six hundred miles an hour, Pops said. How
do you end a poem that's some tiny guy afraid and excited on an airplane?

How do you articulate the speed your life is moving, has moved. How
do you end a poem that's breaking your heart so much so you're crying—

for real—a grown-ass man on a fucking airplane—going
five, six hundred miles an hour because you want to be with her.

And the plane's heading down toward the clouds, jumping a little.
When the poem's in them, you can't, it can't, see anything.

Just a thing inside another thing jumping and jumping and
it's all right there inside itself held in the pocket of something so big,

so much greater than you. It is what it is. And there's no ground
in sight. You're in the clouds with their salt and wet and

the attendant's telling you to turn off your poem,
so the flight's end is the poem's end, almost.

Leaning your face against the clouds, your poem thinks of her cheek
against your beard, knows she'll ask why you're crying.

Your poem's whole life's before and behind it.
Your poem will be standing there holding her, and your heart

will jump inside your chest's pocket, your fingers on her spine.
The tears will be quiet, and you,

you poem you, where everything happens so fast,
you'll say, I want to read you this story I love.

Asylum Seeker Driving through Northwest Arkansas

Where water pools
        one can find a way to live.
How many days
        a man can think of a woman.

If they speak again, Christian hopes
        she'd say, You're fucking killing me
tonight, because she means it
        when she swears.

I'd very much like to feel
        your lips on me, she'd say.
Your hands on my hands,
        Christian would say, ask,

Why'd you say I'm killing you tonight?
        Interpret for yourself, she'd say. Even
this late it happens—When
        Christian Anton Gerard looks

at Arkansas, he sees her words
        in the pause between good and night,
the kiss he blew her once across a field
        speckled with chalk maple, river birch.

It was and was not the last time he saw her.
        The heart is déjà vu. The place memory
lives—river laps against the skull,
        eyes like dams. It's night.

Fuck, you kill me. *My body hums. Fuck. You Kill me,*
        she said. The full moon in Christian
sees what lives in what's welled
        in his throat-river's mouth. Let this

not be an aubade. Let it not have a name.
        In this life, surface tension's all
Christian knows. He's all blues and greens
        glowing. Christian could cry tonight

because years are heavy as water;
        he'll save it in case he sees her
silhouette again, his words east to kind hands.

Preservation

Christian Anton Gerard's tongue is a wetland.
When he moves his lips—Palm Warblers. Thousands.
His tongue's a Venus flytrap trapping itself. It is what it is.
It's because of the girl from Memphis.
Earlier he considered watching the news to catch up
on world events. He lives in a bubble. A white man
in a world with more white men than nitrogen.
That fact may be erroneous. Christian Anton Gerard
has a love/hate relationship with his own politics.
He's more like the German government.
When he thinks of Germany, Christian Anton Gerard
thinks of his great-great-great grandfather who
made shoes for the German king and queen.
Gerard wonders why he's not named Schumacher.
He wishes he were related to Michael Schumacher,
the Formula One racing world everything. But Christian
Anton Gerard is just German. Sort of.
German, Norwegian, and confused. It's because of the girl
in Memphis, on the delta. She's a wetland. It was on the news.
Wetland preservation's so fashionable these days.
Christian Anton Gerard once stood in a wetland at sunset.
He's done it more than once. But once,
there were bird shadow shapes dancing, there were
some whitetail milling about with vigil. There were
bullfrogs and crickets, ducks running on water into dusk.
Once though, Christian Anton Gerard stood in a wetland
at sunset—a fox howl made his heart beat different.

Christian Anton Gerard to Her Sort of in the Style of a Teenaged Love Poem

—after Christian Anton Gerard and Her

I.
What I want to say sits on my lip, a wren
in a rose bush at night, an orange moon huge

and waiting. In the dark, silence is my palm
up to my mouth, all the wishes breathed

out, hanging oak leaves against
your eyes restless in the breeze,

keep me quiet and listening. So I can
follow you wherever you will smile.

II.
Sometimes I hold cloves on my tongue,
pour honey straight in my mouth

when nobody's looking. I did it tonight
for the first time. Three times.

I plan to make it a thing. I've never told anyone this.
Clove sting and honey burn. Fool for you. It's ours. Our doing.

III.
I think of your hands, with which I'm obsessed. Your hands
holding flowers. Your hands holding a knife and fork.

Your right hand rising to your mouth. How, I imagine,

you will not move your eyes from mine as you eat.
Your hands holding a book, the words rising from your mouth.

There are metaphors for this.

You are a heartbeat heard in a breath. You are a smile felt in night.
You are red and red's history.

Color is tricky to pin down. Light, a powerful stallion to break.

Yes, light, a stallion. Have you heard that Highwaymen song
about the silver stallion? No matter. Cat Power's cover is better.

Your hands in mine as it plays. Your thigh's inside against mine

because music works like alfalfa in wind. Your hands
holding my face. My hands holding your back's small.

Two tulips in a vase. No. Two tulips on a mountain's edge. How

holding is organic. Holding on is not a mystery.
How—my hands on your face. Yours on mine.

IV.
I said your name forty-nine times before I fell
asleep last night—my voice fire-pop and invitation.

I am all buzz and zing and you
and yes and you and yes. Yes.

I dreamt your voice. Breath in my ear.
I woke a tulip field at sunrise.

Dear Bob Dylan I'm Not Angry

because when I think *Hard Rain* or *Shelter*
From The Storm I think afraid. Being.

I love those songs.
Probably, you admire some of my poems.

But poet to poet, man, what if the best rain's hard rain?
What if the best shelter's in the best hard rain?

Yesterday a woman said to me, May I drive to you.
A woman said that. To me. And she did.

Bob, I came in from the wilderness. I cleaned
the kitchen for hours, made my bed to lie in.

I came in a creature void of form. But I know
my pastoral, Bob, I've done my homework.

We both know our Sidney and Spenser,
Sannazaro, and we love Dante's love. Look Bob,

this life is bone inside burlap. Look,
Bob, a woman said to me, May I drive to you.

And I said Of course. And she did.
Can we agree there's a wild we never imagined

back where the Muses live? Where if we're lucky we'll be
Belphoebe-hearted Amorette and Scudamore revisions

unseparated by the Faerie Queene? Can we agree
there's nothing but to let her breath be our guide?

Poem with Pursed Lips

—after Her and Wallace Stevens and Walt Whitman

Sure, Wallace Stevens, a dwelling's made
        from air, and in the evening,
                and it can be enough. Should be.

But there's more—She is the evening,
        putting on the garments stitched
                from air coarse and fine and

the stuff of breath—making a man
        both a lone lamb under a tree
                and lightning reminding

light synonyms heaven and earth,
        allowing the lamb's heart its pounding,
                breath, the heartbeat's dwelling—

my eyes' capillaries, my need for closer to the tree.
        What she should know of me—that
                and that. This. How I can look

into her little rooms large enough
        to hold her words, her readers
                and know our *intimate* a house

apart and not. Can I tell
        her I imagine we are both
                air and evening in our one

room I enter at waking, in which
        being is being's definition?

Christian Anton Gerard to Ryan Adams, via Caliban

Let's call it art when I say I'd have sawed off my arm
this evening so I wouldn't have had to move my son
snoring like a lumberjack (which I've always wanted to be
since I read *Sometimes a Great Notion*).

Let's say it's the kind of thing an old man says of his son
because Americans are so masculine-aware, but
any man worth his sweat knows the saw
would wake the son, knows he's got a choice:

Hold the boy while you may or tend what needs tending.
It's each day's worst choice. It's also not a choice,
but a question of need. A man's heart's tended by holding.
That was an artsy riddle because you're Ryan Adams and

you've got the sweetest guitar I've ever seen.
But seriously. Let's play a game. How 'bout
we free associate metaphors. I'll start with a list,
you guess what it's about: Red peony. Red apple. Red voice.

Red and green eyes. Sugar. Shotgun. Red
obvious. Red oblivious. Red breath. Red well-read.
I can't keep it out of my poems like you can't
keep it out of your songs: That thing in our veins,

weird happy in heartbreak and its counterpoint
unabashed like a beautiful Caliban in love.
No. Not a beautiful Caliban. I wouldn't wish Caliban on anyone.
Hell no. Apologies. I tried that allusion thing I like, but it didn't work.

Forget it. We can be straight up. We both love to hold and be held.
When I said *it* I meant what you or I'd crawl over coals for
if we could find it all in one person. Need's answer.
She has a name. I will tell you over dinner.

Christian Anton Gerard to Josh Jones

Europe itself a trumpet trumpeting some key
we could trust. *Megan*, you said so many times
eleven years ago. Jones, I find myself deep in a love affair

with Ryan Adams again (Always). You know how it is.
How it comes on. Us eleven years ago, wanting everything and how

we spoke our wanting. You said *Megan*. I said several names,
the ones I'd named heartbreaker. Do you remember
walking up the train station stairs into Munich

whistling Oh My Sweet Carolina? Our hearts praying
that would be love's city—Love's calling you into

the sea in Nice the night that Moroccan guitar player
sang 'til sunrise and we kept him in wine.
We kept us all in wine. Sea just down

the rocks. George Bush down the street at that hotel.
He made us hate the flags on our packs.

How many times we talked life's constitution.
I'm still sorry for pissing in the Malta girl's boots.
What can I say? Barcelona. Absinthe upon whiskey. Roses.

Jones. Life was upon us then. It's upon me now.
This epistle is proof. I won't forget you standing in love

on that rock just out of the surf in Nice.
That rock's where I stand now. That perfect night. The woman
in the painting. That woman's turned around, Jones. Green eyes.

Each night. Each morning. I see it now, why you said,
Megan. How you couldn't not say *Megan*. Thank you for that.

Christian Anton Gerard to Her

If every poem's a political poem, then so is every heartbeat.
I didn't have my raincoat and I've never bought an umbrella.

Sometimes I get on an airplane, look at my shoes
and wonder, do I want to die in these shoes?

When I think of an epigram, I think of a poem that's more.
In this language *want* is a word that means need.

It feels like the teakettle itself is made of amphetamines.
I'm not culturally authorized to talk about that.

Silence sometimes is all the ear can hold.
Silence is not *I*, but contains multitudes.

Sometimes it's the seventeen minutes you give yourself
when you see your choice like the harvest moon

and you begin figuring how to soberly hold it.
None of this stuff was here before. All the trees were smaller.

I want my sweat to taste like good, good labor, and dirt and grass.
I want my name to taste like that in your mouth.

Dear You, Ideally It Will Go Down Like This:

A guy down the street's got a sixty-four GMC pickup
in his driveway. It's not moved since I moved here.

I left a note on his door asking if I could buy it and
to call me at my number and that I was serious.

But listen. I'm thinking I'll go over there Saturday
('cause there's another car there Saturdays) and knock

that guy's door till he answers. I'll take a six-pack of beer
and a six-pack of pop, and he can pick. I'll pour him one.

I'll ask him to sit on his weathered deck, and we will.
I'll I ask if I may smoke and if he would like to join me.

He will accept my cigarettes, and we'll talk about his lake.
Eventually I'll look at him, and I will say his name.

I'll say, Name, seven months ago I left a note on your door
with my phone number asking if I could buy your truck.

I believe you don't want to sell your truck, and I came here
intending to ask you to buy your truck, but I have another idea.

The Jimmy's in good shape, Name, but it needs tires.
How about you let me buy tires for your truck?

And Name will ask why. Because, Name, this is what I'd like.
I'm in love, Name. She lives four, four and a half hours from here.

I work at the school. I walk to work, the store, you know. But
I need a vehicle, Name, and here's the thing—don't sell your truck

to me or anyone. How about you let me take it to see my love
when I need to? It'll be a lot. As much as she'll let me. As much

cash as I have for gas. But I'll always park it here, and I'll ask you
always if I can take your truck, Name, to go see this woman—

The woman you sit on a dock like this and talk about, Name,
now and for the rest of your life and if you're lucky—

the woman who'll sit out here with you and talk forever. The woman.
That's why I'd like to buy your truck tires and keep buying them.

I'll chart my mileage, and I'll go now, Name,
if you'll hand me those keys. I'll have tires on it tonight.

I'll leave in the morning. You'll wake and the truck'll be gone,
and you'll know you're letting me and your truck live it, Name—

the dream—that woman I'll talk about for the rest of my life
or with the rest of my life. That's where I'm at, Name.

Ideally, Name'll pull the key from his overalls' middle pocket,
hand it to me, tell me to wash it when I get back.

I'll give her white-walls and put a tape deck under the dash.
I'll throw my pack in the back. I'll sleep in the bed. I'll wake at light.

I'll stop at the last payphone I know in existence on the edge of town.
I'll listen to the quarters drop like my heart. I'll say, Hey,

he said yes. I'll be there about noon. I'll say, Hey,
what do you say we stay together a few days, a week maybe?

Let's roll by your favorite record store. Let's buy a tape.
You show me something you think I've never heard.

How 'bout we drive. When the tape's over, we stop in the next town,
we find a record store and buy a tape. If there's no record store,

we hit the gas station tape rack. We make it happen.
Ideally, you'll say, Yes. And I'll say, Hey, I'm coming to you.

Christian Anton Gerard in the Introspective

This time I'm ready to wear the skeleton suit
and smell like a birthday candle. I walk now

a skeleton re-wrought because of one woman.
It's like Peire Vidal wearing the fur of the wolf,

and the shepherd's dogs / have run [him] to earth.
You know the rest—how he was left for dead, how

for one woman, the wolf fur, the seeing what is not
there, the breathing its day, the asking where were you.

Forever I found that saddest line. But, no. Throw a brick
through the other guy's window (then pay for it).

Cicadas unearth themselves after three hundred years.
Someone's boot will lay undisturbed on the ocean floor

after this reckoning is reckoned. There's a picture
of a boot like that in a book called *Titanic*.

That picture's stayed with me since second grade.
What remains. What remains after reckoning.

I'm saying maybe Vidal saw her everywhere,
maybe he means she'd been there the whole time.

I asked, at first, the same question each day about H,
but I was a wolf pup playing at passion.

Vidal though, my brother, you wore your own skin.
Your own heart, that tender thing. It had to be.

I know because I stand before her. Peire, in my heart,
I see my mouth in spring float away on the river,

which gives me leave to tell her I am hers
and I am in my own skin. A wolf's

not vicious. A wolf loves the right way,
killing what it must to feed what life wills.

Notes

"The Poet Making a Scene"
   Edmund Spenser's entrance into this poem centers on *The Faerie Queene's* character Calidore, who notoriously interrupts others throughout the poem. The italicized lines are directly borrowed from *The Faerie Queene.*

"Whiskey Called. She Said,"
   This poem was born out of rumination on T.S. Eliot's "East Coker" and my alcoholism.

"Irises"
   The poem's epigraph is from the prayer, "God, grant me the serenity to accept the things I cannot change, the courage to change the things I can, and the wisdom to know the difference," written by Reinhold Niebuhr. Neibuhr used the prayer during his sermons as early as 1934 and it appeared in a magazine in 1951. The Matthew Dickman Poem quoted is titled "Trouble."

"Pointed"
   The poem's epigraph is from the prayer, "God, grant me the serenity to accept the things I cannot change, the courage to change the things I can, and the wisdom to know the difference," written by Reinhold Niebuhr. Neibuhr used the prayer during his sermons as early as 1934 and it appeared in a magazine in 1951. Bill Wilson was one of the founders of the program called Alcoholics Anonymous and the reference to him appears in his story within the book *Alcoholics Anonymous.*

"Steelhead Don't Ask Where The White Goes"
   The poem's epigraph is from the prayer, "God, grant me the serenity to accept the things I cannot change, the courage to change the things I can, and the wisdom to know the difference," written by Reinhold Niebuhr. Neibuhr used the prayer during his sermons as early as 1934 and it appeared in a magazine in 1951.

"For a Poet Who Fears His Elegies Are Too Sentimental"
   This poem is dedicated to poet Michael C. Peterson and his family.

"Twenty-Something Poet Making a Mix Tape"
> The poem references musical artists PM Dawn, Prince, Otis Redding, and Madonna alongside the musicals *Rent* and *West Side Story*, and the poets Walt Whitman, Aphra Behn, John Donne, Sir Thomas Wyatt, John Milton and John Wilmot, Second Earl of Rochester.

"Because there are Nights that Seem to Put One Arm First"
> This poem makes use of Michel de Montaigne's ideas on the essay as an "attempt."

"Image"
> The poem references John Keats' notion of "Negative Capability."

"Materials; or Revision"
> The poem makes reference to Robert Frost's poem, "Home Burial."

"Operator's Manual"
> The poem makes reference to Vladimir Nabokov's novel *Pnin* and borrows "ecstatic prose" from John Updike's blurb on the novel's back cover. "I'll be the man who ran against the wind and won," references Bob Seger's song, "Against the Wind," and the poem's last line is borrowed from Taj Mahal's song "Lovin' in My Baby's Eyes."

"Usable Past"
> This poem borrows its last four lines from Sir Philip Sidney's *Astrophil & Stella Sonnet* 25.

"Permission"
> Sir Joshua Reynolds was a prominent 18th century painter. The reference and citation in this poem comes from his Discourses on Art, which were originally composed as lectures delivered to students at the Royal Academy of Arts between 1769 and 1776.

"Anonymous"
> The poem's form is borrowed from Dylan Thomas' syllabic poem, "Poem in October."

"Christian Anton Gerard To Scalise From New Orleans"
> The style of the epistle's title is borrowed from David Biespiel's epistles in *Charming Gardners*.

"To Ansel on His Second Birthday"
  The poem references Jackson Browne's song, "I Thought I Was A Child."

"Poem with Madrigals"
  The lines "rationality is not unnecessary. It serves the chaos of knowledge. It serves feeling," are borrowed from Adrienne Rich's interview with Audre Lorde on August 30, 1979. The full interview can be found in *Conversations with Audre Lorde*, edited by Joan Wylie Hall. "Ezra Pound, Ezra Pound, make it new, make it new" references Pound's book by the same title, *Make It New*.

"Still Life With Myself Two Years Six Months Sober"
  The poem's line, "Cut off the heads and tales from my past's dead weight" is a variant of a line in W.S. Merwin's poem, "Peire Vidal."

"Poetry Can Save The World?"
  This poem references Mary Oliver's poem "What I Have Learned so Far." The poem also makes reference to Danté's Beatrice and *Inferno* alongside Charles Bukowski's *Love Is a Dog from Hell*.

"Defense of Poetry; or Alcoholic Expected Home"
  This poem references Symphosius' twelfth riddle, which I first encountered in Bin Ramke's poem, "Birds Fly Through Us."

"Defense of Poetry; or Prayer in Recovery"
  The poem's epigraph is from Ben Jonson's "On My First Sonne."

"Water Skiing with Robert Creeley"
  This poem was inspired by the cover photo on Creeley's *Selected Poems* 1945-2005, in which he is shown driving a small boat. The words in quotation marks: "there, and there" and "what one wants is / what one wants, yet complexly" are borrowed from Creeley's poem "For W.C.W."

"Defense of Poetry; or Love Prayer Prayed By Christian Anton Gerard"
  The line "our bones green embers" is an incarnation of an image in James Wright's poem, "The Jewel," where he writes, "…When I stand upright in the wind, / My bones turn into dark emeralds."

"Defense of Poetry"
  This poem references Rilke's *The Book of Images*. The poem alluded

to at my poem's end is Rilke's "Evening," though I confused, in memory, Rilke's image of the evening putting on its garments with the image of the world unbuttoning its blouse, which appears in Stephen Dunn's poem, "The Routine Things Around the House."

"Christian Anton Gerard Thinking He's Milton's Adam"

John Milton's *Paradise Lost* is the main poetic contact point for this poem, but Spenser's Red Cross Knight is also included in the third stanza in conversation with my reading of Milton's Adam and Eve looking out from the gates Eden.

"Sublime Prayer For An Alcoholic"

The idea and tone for this poem came after re-reading Edmund Burke's "Philosophical Enquiry into the Origin of Our Ideas of the Sublime and Beautiful." The poem also features the "Duende" as a character. Duende is generally understood to be an idea of "soul" in a work of art. Frederico Garcia Lorca heavily explored the idea in his lecture, "Play and Theory of the Duende." Here, I have made use of Duende as a guiding force for my meditation and fiction making.

"Confession of the Poet who Brought Books into a Public Restroom"

This poem makes multiple poetic references and allusions. Early in the poem, I reference my own work in speaking of the character "Wilmot," who is a major figure in my first book, and who is based on the persona of John Wilmot, Second Earl of Rochester—notorious Restoration Libertine poet and thinker. The poem also makes use of Liam Rector's poem, "I Get a Feeling" and Gerald Stern's "In Memory of W.H. Auden." The italicized lines are borrowed from each poet's poem. This poem also makes use of Spencer's stanzaic formulation used in *The Faerie Queene*, which I found quite useful in helping to emphasize the poem's experience as my speaker's own allegorization.

"You've Spotted Him In The Restaurant"

This poem references Mark Strand's poem, "Breath."

"A Knife's Signature in his Alcoholic Palms"

This poem alludes to William Shakespeare's 1594 narrative poem, "The Rape of Lucrece."

"Pastoral: Can We Say Cowboy Anymore?"
> The lines "The wise are above / books. It is for the General sort that we write" are borrowed from Samuel Daniels' *A Defence of Ryme*.

"Or Dear John Ashbery"
> This poem responds to John Ashbery's "Some Trees" and borrows the line, "a canvas on which emerges a chorus of smiles."

"Defense of Poetry; or Poem in which I can't Imagine My Own Death"
> This poem references and borrows lines from Jill Rosser's "Revisiting the City of Her Birth," Edward Hirsch's poem "Special Orders," and Mark Halliday's poem "Chicken Salad."

"Holdfast"
> "Behind all this some great happiness is hiding" is borrowed from Yehuda Amichai's poem, "Memorial Day for the War Dead."

"Christian Anton Gerard, A Shearsman of Sorts"
> The poem makes reference to and borrows from Wallace Stevens' *The Man with the Blue Guitar*.

"Sobering Interrogative: A Man's Most Vulnerable"
> Stephen Dunn's line, "…Let love when it can / be a form of containment" is borrowed from his poem "Bad Plants."

"Christian Anton Gerard Moving Toward Psalm"
> The poem's epigraph is borrowed from William Shakespeare's *Romeo and Juliet*.

"Defense of Poetry; or The Alcoholic's Imitation"
> The lines "The greatest natural genius cannot subsist / on its own stock; he who resolves never to ransack any mind / but his own, will soon be reduced, from mere bareness, to / the poorest of all imitations," are taken from Joshua Reynolds' *Discourses on Art*.

"Defense Prayer"
> This poem borrows and modifies the lines, "cartography through the silences," "How do I exist?," "If there is a poetry where this could happen," and "not as blank spaces, / or whispers as words stretched like skin / over meanings, but as silence falls / at the end of a night through which two people have talked till dawn," from

Adrienne Riche's "Cartographies of Silence" in *The Dream of a Common Language.*

"Enargeia"
"Enargeia" in Sir Philip Sidney's spelling and use in his *Defence of Poesy* is "a forcibleness" of the passions exhibited in a work of fiction.

"Christian Anton Gerard And Her Yet Without A Past"
The poem makes early reference to Cyndi Lauper's song "Girls Just Wanna Have Fun" and the movie *The Goonies.* The poem's last line is borrowed from H.D.'s poem, "Night." The original lines read, "The night has cut / each from each…"

"Defense of Poetry; or How To Say The Heart's Epitome"
This poem responds to John Milton's *Paradise Lost* and borrows the lines, "they hand in hand with wand'ring / steps and slow, through Eden / took their solitary way" and "four streams' / murmuring waters fall and / the fringed bank is with myrtle crowned."

"Christian Anton Gerard To Her Sort Of In The Style Of A Teenaged Love Poem"
The line "I am all buzz and zing and you" is indebted to Anne Sexton's poem, "The Kiss."

"Poem with Pursed Lips"
This poem responds to and borrows lines from Wallace Stevens' poem, "Final Soliloquy of the Interior Paramour" and from Walt Whitman's poem, "Song of Myself."

"Christian Anton Gerard To Ryan Adams, via Caliban"
This poem alludes to Ken Kesey's novel *Sometimes a Great Notion* and the character Caliban from William Shakespeare's play *The Tempest.*

"Christian Anton Gerard To Josh Jones"
This poem references Ryan Adams' song, "Oh My Sweet Carolina" from his record *Heartbreaker.*

"Christian Anton Gerard In The Introspective"
This poem references W.S. Merwin's poem, "Peire Vidal" and Wes Anderson's movie *The Royal Tenenbaums* (specifically, when Royal says, "Throw a brick through the other guy's window").

Grateful acknowledgment is made to the editors and staffs of the following journals in which these poems first appeared, sometimes with different titles:

"Holdfast: My Alcoholic Head in Recovery" in *The Adroit Journal*
"Christian Anton Gerard Thinking He's Milton's Adam" in *Apt*
"Permission" in *Apt*
"Pointed" in *Apt*
"Twenty-Something Poet Made A Mix Tape" in *B O D Y*
"Materials; or Revision" in *Bluestem*
"Aubade in Afternoon" in *Cleaver*
"Christian Anton Gerard and Her Yet Without a Past" in *The Collagist*
"Her and Christian Anton Gerard in an Argon Cloud" in *The Collagist*
"Operator's Manual" in *The Collagist*
"Water Skiing with Robert Creeley" in *The Collagist*
"Poem with Madrigals" in *Cutthroat*
"Pastoral: Can We Say Cowboy Anymore?" in *Cutthroat*
"Dear You, Ideally It Will Go Down Like This" in *Diode*
"To Ansel on His Second Birthday" in *Diode*
"A Knife's Signature in His Alcoholic Palms" in *Epiphany*
"Defense of Poetry; or Alcoholic Expected Home" in *Epiphany*
"Defense of Poetry; or Prayer in Recovery" in *Epiphany*
"Anonymous" in *Fjords Review*
"Preservation" in *The Literary Review*
"Whiskey Called. She Said," in *The Literary Review*
"Rhinoceri Believe in a Golden Age for Love" in *Pank*
"Christian Anton Gerard to Her" in *The Pinch*
"Sobering Interrogative: A Man's Most Vulnerable" in *The Pinch*
"Defense of Poetry" in *Post Road*
"Defense of Poetry; or Poem with Bowling Leagues and Black Dresses" in *Post Road*
"Christian Anton Gerard is Unable to be Opaque" in *Review Americana*
"You've Spotted Him in the Restaurant" in *Stirring: A Literary Collection*
"Ars Poetica" in *storySouth*
"Image" in *The Tattooed Poets Project*
"Steelhead Don't Ask Where the White Goes" in *Thrush*
"Christian Anton Gerard in the Introspective" in *Thrush*
"Christian Anton Gerard Moving Toward Psalm" in *Thrush*
"Blood is no More Life than a Cloud Resembling a Goose is a Goose" in *Thrush*
"Defense of Poetry; or The Poet Explaining Himself" in *Thrush*
"Defense Prayer" in *The Zen Space*
"Enargeia" in *The Zen Space*

Thank you to my love, Heather Dobbins, for all you have given to these poems, this life, the color red and me.

Thank you, Ansel, for you—for being my best guy.

Thank you to my parents, Dedra Gerard and Stephen Gerard, for your unwavering support and love. Infinite thanks are due to the following friends who have seen these poems and this book (and me) through in part or in full in every possible capacity: Helen Stead Bentz, Paula Bohince, Dexter L. Booth, Katie Burnett, Katherine Davis, Jamie Dickson, Stephanie Dugger, Tarfia Faizullah, Natalia Holtzman, Charlotte Pence, Todd Ridley, Josh Robbins, Mike Scalise, Karen Schubert, Erin Elizabeth Smith, Carolyn Stice and Giuseppe Taurino.

I am greatly indebted to my teachers, mentors and colleagues for their support, expertise, encouragement, guidance, advice and friendship: Misty Anderson, Steven Bauer, Michael Collier, Joel Davis, Kathryn DeZur, Annie Finch, Linda Gregerson, Joe Hardin, Sean Henry, Rachel Hile, Ed Hirsch, Jane Hirshfield, Denna Iammarino, Luisa A. Igloria, Richard Jackson, Roger Kuin, Marilyn Kallet, Sandy Longhorn, Rosario Nolasco-Schultheiss, Ron Offen, Tim O'Keefe, Janet Peery, Carl Phillips, Anne Lake Prescott, Beth Quitslund, Jim Reiss, Sheri Reynolds, William Pitt Root, Ernest Rufleth, Tim Seibles, Art Smith, Mike Smith, Brian Spears, Robert Stillman, Andy Strycharski, Cammie Sublette, Pam Uschuk, Ellen Bryant Voigt and Laura Witherington.

Thank you to my students at the University of Tennessee and the University of Arkansas-Fort Smith for challenging me and for helping shape so many of the ways these poems were written, especially: Lissa Brooks, Kari Carbajal, Callie Craig, Ben Cullen, Laken Emerson, Cheyenne C. Fletcher, Jamie Fore, Ahna Fryhover, Liz Harms, Laura Hawkins, Damien Irwin, Nick Morrissey, Darcy Parker, Colby Post, Nahia Riviera and Brooke Slaton.

Special thanks to Nicky Beer, Emma Bolden, Brian Brodeur, Geffrey Davis, Sean Thomas Dougherty, Daryl Farmer, Amorak Huey, Terry Kennedy, Peter LaBerge, Shara Lessley, Al Maginnes, Andrew McFadyen-Ketchum, Matthew Olzmann, Molly Bass Rector, Jeremy Michael Reed, Barbara Sabol, Ed Skoog, Molly Spencer and Dana Staves for your time, kindness and effort in helping usher this book into the world.

I would like to thank the Bread Loaf Writers' Conference, the Prague Summer Program, the Sundress Academy for the Arts, the Miami University English and Creative Program, the Old Dominion University English and Creative Writing Program, and the University of Tennessee English and Creative Writing Program for community and guidance during many of these poems' beginnings, middles, and ends, as well as for the enduring friendships that have seen me through.

OTHER C&R PRESS TITLES

FICTION

Ivy vs. Dogg
by Brian Leung

A History of the Cat In Nine Chapters or Less
by Anis Shivani

While You Were Gone
by Sybil Baker

Spectrum
by Martin Ott

That Man in Our Lives
by Xu Xi

SHORT FICTION

Meditations on the Mother Tongue
by An Tran

The Protester Has Been Released
by Janet Sarbanes

ESSAY AND CREATIVE NONFICTION

Immigration Essays
by Sybil Baker

Je suis l'autre: Essays and Interrogations
by Kristina Marie Darling

Death of Art
by Chris Campanioni

POETRY

Negro Side of the Moon
by Early Braggs

Holdfast
by Christian Anton Gerard

Ex Domestica
by E.G. Cunningham

Collected Lies and Love Poems
by John Reed

Imagine Not Drowning
by Kelli Allen

Les Fauves
by Barbara Crooker

Tall as You are Tall Between Them
by Annie Christain

The Couple Who Fell to Earth
by Michelle Bitting

CHAPBOOKS

Cuntstruck by Kate Northrop

Relief Map by Erin Bertram

Love Undefined by Jonathan Katz

CPSIA information can be obtained
at www.ICGtesting.com
Printed in the USA
LVOW10s0432200218
567244LV00002B/181/P